*To a friend –
This 'book' becomes a new
beginning of spiritual insights
for you!
    Paul McKinley*

Rules of the Spirit
Integrating Spiritual Truths in Daily Living

Paul McKinley

AM-PM Publishing

AM-PM Publishing
116 Charles St.
Gordonsville VA 22942

Copyright © 2015 by Paul McKinley
First paperback printing January 2016

All rights reserved. This book may not be reproduced in whole or in part, stored in a retrieval system, or transmitted in any form or by any means electronic, mechanical, or other without written permission from the publisher, except by a reviewer, who may quote brief passages in a review.

ISBN 978-0-9971198-0-0

Contents

Testimonials	ix
Acknowledgements	xi
Foreword	xiii
Chapter 1: Dawning of Insight	1
Chapter 2: Turning an Agnostic into a Spiritualist	9
Chapter 3: A New Paradigm for Living	19
Chapter 4: The Reality Inversion: Forgiveness and Apology	31
Chapter 5: The Half-Truth	45
Chapter 6: The Insanity of Fear	57
Chapter 7: Scarcity Mindset: The Fall from Eden	67
Chapter 8: The Law of Attraction	81
Chapter 9: Right and Wrong, Good and Evil	99
Chapter 10: Spiritual Stages	107
Chapter 11: Next Steps	113
About the Author	115

There is no such thing as curses in life.
There are only blessings that we may choose
not to enjoy much at the time.
-- Paul McKinley

For Mike,
The end of your journey became the beginning of mine.

For Ann,
Who encourages me, who blesses me with her own insights, and acts as my sounding board for the ideas that became this book – and beyond.

For My Spiritual Brothers and Sisters at Unity of Temple
For being my guinea-pigs as I began to present these ideas, and for encouraging me to write this book.

Testimonials

"As a frequent guest speaker at Unity of Temple, Paul's messages were always looked to with anticipation and joy. As he'd slow-walk the group through various concepts of being, in short order, the congregation would be silently nodding their heads in full agreement. From his messages came deeper perspectives on truth and how it relates to common everyday events. Albeit likely unnoticed by most at the time, Paul was dropping seed and supplying spiritual nourishment that, even today, produces meaningful impact in the lives of those who frequent the little Unity church in the heart of Central Texas."
-- Russell Jones, US Army Ret.

"As a notable resource of knowledge for daily living, Paul takes one on a journey into Spirit by providing simple eye-opening concepts, enhancing understanding and facilitating the practical application of spiritual principles. Typical thinking expands as one is inspired to delve deeper and draw from Spirit, the strength and power to be true expressions of our greater selves."
-- Mary Parrish, Author of *Be Still and Know, Meditation for Beginners*
Co-Author with Lisa Nichols of *Living Proof: Celebrating the Gifts That Came Wrapped in Sandpaper*

Acknowledgements

First of all, I'd like to give thanks to Raymond Aaron, whose 10-10-10 program provided both the framework and impetus that helped me get this book done. I had started writing bits and pieces before I came across his program, but I would probably still just be thinking about it rather than getting it done. There are lots of mentors out there; Raymond is distinguished from others by his integrity.

Many years ago, I was encouraged to speak by Jim Chandler, then senior pastor of Round Rock First United Methodist Church in Round Rock, Texas. Jim trusted me to speak the truth. Ultimately that led to my becoming a Layspeaker, and things have evolved from that point.

My wife Ann has also provided encouragement and insights that help along the way. It's been a long process, but she's been there for me and provided the gentle accountability along the way.

Finally, there have been too many friends to list, from my spiritual community, who have encouraged me to write this book with their questions of "When are you going to write a book about this?"

Foreword

Even though I have become known as a master speaker and distinguished success mentor, my education is in the sciences. As such, I understand the usual gap between the scientific mind and the mysticism that goes along with discussions of spiritually based topics. The two don't usually go together – science-minded people tend to want to work with things they can measure, and this is inherently difficult for spiritual topics.

Paul McKinley's education as a mechanical engineer certainly qualifies him as a science and technically-minded individual. Even so, he is able to leverage his logic to present spiritual topics in a way that makes the subject interesting and understandable, even to science-minded individuals who would normally avoid spiritual topics.

This book is a collection of unique insights gained over the years, in many cases by living through difficult and painful events. Rather than being barriers, however, those events became the springboard for insights and ways of understanding spiritual topics that can apply to everyday situations.

I strongly recommend this book, to science-minded and spiritually based people alike!

Raymond Aaron, New York Times Best-selling Author

Chapter 1
Dawning of Insight

"To believe with certainty, we must begin with doubting."
— Stanislaus I

Beginnings

I was raised in a Christian environment, and schooled in the Christian traditions and mindshare. Christianity is my tradition: it is what I know. Therefore my writing is mostly from a Christian point of view and uses Christian symbols, references and ideas.

I do not apologize for my Christian tradition. However, unlike many Christians, I do not hold Christianity as being "the only way." I believe God comes to us wherever we are, in ways that will be meaningful to us in our own land, our own culture, our own tradition. After all, if you believe that God creates all things, then it follows that all lands, cultures, and traditions are also created by God and that God would present God's self to the different cultures and traditions in ways that would have meaning in the context of those cultures and traditions. What is important is our connection to our divine roots: the Spirit from which we come, not the frame of reference by which we develop that connection.

I invite you, the reader, to translate the concepts and ideas presented in this book into the "language" of your tradition. If the concepts and ideas I present contain truth, and if you can look past the language I use to present them, the truth will become evident to you and you may achieve enlightenment that you might not otherwise. It won't matter whether you align yourself with Christian, Muslim, Buddhist, Hindi, or any other spiritual tradition.

I consider myself to be a "Spiritualist," not a "Religionist." I believe that a focus on spiritual truths will always lead to the highest good. Many people in the modern age have become disillusioned with spiritual concepts because, at least in the Western culture that I'm familiar with, the spiritual concepts are usually wrapped in the robes of Religion. While Religion can be a good introduction to the Spiritual, the character of Religion is not "of the Spirit" – it is based on what I call "Rules of the World" – a concept we'll explore in this book. Religion's basis in the Rules of the World produces difficulties which eventually turn people away.

I believe modern denominations would do well to heed this disillusionment with the worldly Religion and find ways to nourish and support the spark of the Spirit within their congregations and community, in ways that hold true to Spiritual, not Religious, truths.

In The World, Not Of The World

A number of years ago I became intrigued by the phrase "We are in the world, but not of the world." This is a pretty common saying; I would expect that most people who follow mainstream Christian traditions would recognize the phrase. I believe the concept is pervasive in other traditions as well.

The dichotomy of this phrase begs the question: if we are IN the world, but not OF the world, then where - or what - ARE we OF? What does it mean to be NOT of the world? These questions became the seed for a new paradigm and understanding for living a discerning, spiritual life, which is described in this book.

If we are IN the world, but not OF the world, where are we OF? My answer to this question is that we are of SPIRIT – we are Spirit beings, not Material. Pinch your arm – does that substance you feel between your fingers define what or who you really are? I would say no, that is just a construct, a creation. This answer is based on my understanding of life, which is of course based on my experiences.

As I continued to think about this phrase and what it means, I began to recognize that, while we live our lives in the material world, the world can have an influence on the way we behave, which may or may not line up with our true, spiritual existence. It also challenged my understanding of Reality. Richard Bach used the analogy of a movie theater for describing our material existence. When you go to see a movie, you go into the theater, sit down and, for the moment, put aside your own reality for the fictional reality of the movie. You feel the excitement and pain of the actors on the screen; the images become real. After a while the movie is over, the lights come up and you wipe the matter from your eyes and file out to rejoin the "real" world waiting for you outside. It seems to me that life is like that – we forget for a brief moment of a lifetime about who we really are. The laws that apply to the fictional storyline have little to do with our basic reality.

Exploring the Origins

I asked Rev. David Adkins, who at the time was Senior Pastor of First United Methodist Church in Round Rock TX, if he knew where it came from – his response was that "It sounds kinda Ephesiany." I tried to look up the phrase in various digital versions of the Bible, and although I found verses similar to it, there was no match. There are verses where Jesus refers to himself and his disciples as being "not of this world." There are also verses attributed to the Apostle Paul that refer to living "in the world." My current understanding is that this phrase is traditional liturgy that was in common practice in the 19th century, which means it was used in worship services and prayers as well as statements of faith. While it is not a scriptural quote, it is a paraphrase of scripture – a condensing of a concept that runs through the Protestant Christian New Testament. It is a common phrase in the Christian mindshare. It is used in Christian teaching to encourage the spiritual student to examine their thoughts and behaviors in a different context than the habitual pattern of the world around them. It encourages conscious living, and, to a degree, conscious living based on an example.

What does it say about Who We Are?

What meaning does the phrase "In the world, but not of the world" have with respect to Who We Are? Frankly, the saying could have any number of meanings. An agnostic or atheist might interpret it to mean that we are descended from an alien race. That might be interesting! I believe the more common interpretation is, as I mentioned earlier, that we are of Spirit – expatriot aliens or not. Our real nature is of a substance or character that cannot be measured or quantified in the material world. The laws of the material world don't apply to us, or at least they apply only to the extent that we allow them. In fact it has been my observation that space and time have no meaning in Spirit. I read somewhere that it had been proven that "energy" healing methodologies are not constrained by the speed of light – that whatever is done in one location is instantly manifested in another without the delay that would normally be associated with the "laws of physics" as we know them.

Distance also has no effect either, in time or in effectiveness. It doesn't matter whether the person being treated is in the same room as the healer, or miles or worlds away. There is a good example of this in the biblical story of the Centurion who came to Jesus seeking healing for his servant. The servant "was healed at that moment" without Jesus having to go to the centurion's home or wherever the servant was located. It didn't matter where the servant was.

What does it say about how we could live?

The thing that's really interesting about being NOT Of The World is that it suggests that there is a whole different way of thinking about the way we live. Just as Spirit is not held to the "laws" of physics, so also could the way we live, the way we think, and the way we interact with one another be based on an entirely different set of rules and concepts. The laws of physics appear from a worldly view to be immutable, meaning that they apply in all circumstances. However I have already shown how they do not apply to spirit action: the laws of physics are true for the world, but they are not true for spirit. What else of what we believe and accept from the world does not apply to Spirit? How do Spirit rules apply in worldly situations? When there is a conflict between the ways and methods of the world and the ways and methods of the spirit, which one wins out? How do we decide what is worldly and what is of the spirit? How do we begin to integrate these truths into how we live, and what is the outcome if we do? What is the incentive for adopting this way of thinking and behaving?

What does it say about our Future?

We all know that each of us will pass away from this life at some point. If the spiritual life is real, if we are truly Of The Spirit, it follows that we will return to that realm. All of the things that pertain to the World will become of no consequence – because they weren't ever really "real."

If the World's viewpoint isn't real, then how did we fall into a state of subscribing to a whole set of beliefs that aren't really real? I mention in Chapter 7 the story of Adam and Eve, which I believe to be the metaphorical story of how mankind came to imbibe or "take in" the concept of Good and Evil, of Abundance and Scarcity. Before the "Fall," Mankind, through Adam and Eve, had no concept of Evil, but only of Good. They had no concept of Scarcity. But through absorbing these concepts, which are false concepts by the way, it has colored the mindshare and behavior of Mankind ever since. It's like a virus that, once contracted, can never be fully eliminated from the body.

Due to the presence of the Law of Attraction, if you hold the concept of scarcity in your mindset, then scarcity is what you will produce in your environment. So, it's like a self-fulfilling prophesy – if you think about scarcity, if you fear scarcity, if you put a great deal of energy into scarcity by trying to avoid it, what do you get? More Scarcity!

Good and Evil are somewhat similar to Scarcity and Abundance, except that Good and Evil aren't something you create; they are really just a reflection of your perception. Things you like or approve are "Good," while things you don't like are "Evil." The same Law of Attraction applies, however: as you put energy into labeling something as Evil, as you rail against what is Evil, as you feel the strong negative emotions about that which is Evil, guess what? You are creating more things and circumstances in your life that you will perceive to be "Evil." I will discuss the topic of Good and Evil further in Chapter 9 so that you will better understand the concept that Good and Evil are perception-based.

Rules of the Spirit

The bottom line, though, is that over the millennia, as humankind has better come to understand our spiritual roots, we are moving more and more back towards an Eden life. It may seem to you that there are a lot of evil (there's that perception again) things happening in the contemporary world. However, if you compare life as we know it today to that of a thousand years ago, or two or three thousand years ago, it's possible to see how we as mankind have progressed. Two hundred years ago, slavery was commonplace, while today it is considered criminal. Two thousand years ago crucifixion was a common means of executing someone. Today we're moving towards a concept that no form of execution is valid. If you look for them, there are many other indications that mankind is evolving towards a more spiritual existence in the worldly environment.

Chapter 2
Turning an Agnostic into a Spiritualist

"The great thing in this world is not so much where we stand as in what direction we are moving."
— Oliver Wendell Holmes Sr.

Being raised Christian

I was raised in a Christian family. We went to church regularly. It's natural for a child to accept the things in their environment, and as such I accepted the religion of my family.

However, as I approached teenage years I began to be less fulfilled by the religion experience. My family became less satisfied with the church we were attending and drifted away, eventually ceasing to go to church.

Jesus Freaks

This drifting away was solidified by experiences I had in High School. I suppose every High School student body naturally separates into social sub-groups. We had the social climbers, the hippies, and "kickers" or cowboy/country types. We also had a subgroup we called the "Jesus Freaks." You could easily tell who was a Jesus Freak – they always had a Bible on the top of the stack of books they carried. They would also come up to you, nose high in the air and state "I'm Saved" in a tone that also conveyed their real message: "YOU'RE DAMNED."

Paul McKinley

Now I had a few problems with that attitude. Their idea of being "saved" was that they had accepted Jesus. That's fine; if they want to believe that, I have no problem with that. My own personal view was that I don't get to decide whether I'm saved or not. The best I can do is to do the best I can do and trust that God will fulfill his covenant. The promise is there, and the expectation is there, but it's just not up to me. But to tell me that in a way that implies that they are better than I am, without their even knowing who I am and what my beliefs are, tells me unequivocally that it's all a façade, a farce. It's just another form of social climbing – giving the appearance that one person is better than another, attempting to push oneself up by pushing others down. I believe it's also a fairly solid example of pridefulness, an attitude discouraged by most if not all Spiritual traditions, and especially Christian teaching. To take on the attitude of condescension towards others is distinctly contrary to true Christian teaching and as such underscored the hypocrisy. Remember, I came from a Christian tradition and knew what followed Christian teaching and what didn't.

Now as an adult I recognize the behavior as being a way to compensate for very poor self-esteem, but at the time it just rubbed my nose in the hypocrisy of the Religion of Christianity. If that's what it meant to be Christian, I wanted no part of it. Would-be evangelists take note – be careful that your efforts aren't working against your stated goal by alienating the very people you're trying to reach. The result of this experience was that I became an agnostic, teetering on the brink of atheistic.

Befuddling a Jesus Freak

There is a funny story that comes out of this Jesus Freak thing. During my senior year, I had an English teacher who was a college professor. She had just moved to my hometown with her husband, and had not been able to find a college faculty position, so she took the position teaching high school English. She taught the class just like she would have taught a college class. I loved her as a teacher; she was one of the bright spots of my senior year. Actually, considering that I took only English and a work-study class in the spring semester, that didn't leave much else to compare.

The English class was right before the lunch period, and there were a number of students in the class, including me, who participated in a work-study program where they would go to school in the morning and work a job in the afternoon. So this class was their last class for the day, and some of them would have to leave early when the school schedule shifted late occasionally. I worked as a mechanic at a motorcycle shop, and never had to leave early.

There was a goodly group of social climbers in the class, kids who were used to being coddled by the teachers. This teacher simply did not coddle them. If they wanted to listen and learn, fine. If not, they could do whatever they wanted, provided they did not distract the rest of the class. The teacher would physically turn to the students who were listening and direct her teaching towards them, ignoring the others. Since much of the grade in the class was based on the lecture, they got a nasty surprise when the report cards came. Interestingly enough, after the first grading period they were shocked and complained bitterly about their poor grades, but continued the dysfunctional behavior nonetheless.

Finally there was, you guessed it, a Jesus Freak in the class. He was not one of the 'Climbers who spent their time in idle gossip, however. He sat next to a Mormon girl and me. The Mormon girl knew the Bible backwards and forwards, and I was good at arguing, so between the two of us we kept the poor Jesus Freak busy while devoting at least half our attention to class.

The Jesus Freak also suffered poor grades in the class while the Mormon girl and I did fine. Imagine the fundamentalist Jesus Freak trying to evangelize a Mormon! I would feel sorry for him, except that he had the choice the whole time to let the subject drop and pay attention – it was his own pridefulness that got in the way of his learning.

Confronting Death

I considered myself an agnostic/atheist into my college years, when a tragic event occurred that changed the course of my spiritual journey. My brother Mike was killed in a helicopter "accident." Mike was finishing up his PhD in Geology, and had taken a job with an oil company. He and his wife and 16 month old son had moved to Houston, and Mike was supervising logging of oil wells as they were drilled. He was with a group riding in a helicopter to a drilling platform in the Gulf of Mexico at night, and the pilot flew the helicopter into the water. My brother, an excellent swimmer, drowned. He is the only sibling with whom I had a relationship worth maintaining.

There were two pivotal things that came out of that tragedy. First, it forced me to confront my spiritual beliefs. Secondly, it brought information to my attention that gave "feet" to the spiritual re-evaluation. The two are really connected – if I hadn't been forced to re-evaluate my beliefs, I would not have been receptive to the other information. Like Douglas Adams' "Somebody Else's Problem," the new information would simply have been invisible to me even had I been presented with it. Effectively my turning to the spiritual path was triggered by, and might not have happened without, the tragedy of my brother's passing.

I mentioned that I was at the time agnostic, verging on atheist. One might call an atheist or agnostic a "materialist," meaning they believe only in the material manifestation that they see and understand. Without an understanding of spiritual existence, one can only expect that death means annihilation – the end of the essence of Who We Are. Without the body to support it, the "Observer" we think of as our consciousness simply ceases to exist, leaving only the body as evidence. I was resigned to this understanding: if that was the way it was, then so be it. I was quite reconciled to my own annihilation.

When my brother died, I found that I could not accept my brother's annihilation. It's amazing how a loved one's life can mean more to you than your own, isn't it? Hold that thought; it will fit in later in this book.

So if I was to understand that death isn't really THE END, I had to come to a whole new realization of what life is all about, to re-examine all of my beliefs and understandings about spiritual concepts.

Evidence of Beyond

One thing that pushed me along was what happened with my dad the night my brother died. My dad had occasional migraine headaches. They would get so bad sometimes that my dad (an MD) would inject himself with morphine to ease the pain, and the morphine would make him violently sick – I always said it made him "throw up his toenails." I've never had a headache that was bad enough that I'd rather be violently sick, so I have no concept of how bad his headaches must have been. The night that Mike died, my dad was having one of his *really bad headaches*. At about the same time as Mike died, his headache instantly vanished. No morphine, it was just gone. That never happened before or since. Something happened there that was connected to my brother's death.

Paul McKinley

The next thing that influenced my journey was a book that my parents came across: "Life After Life" by Raymond Moody, MD. This book, and his follow-up book "The Light Beyond," describe Dr. Moody's collected research into something called a "Near Death Experience" or NDE – things that people experience when they are clinically dead and are revived. These books were of course very helpful with the grief I felt at my brother's passing. They gave me a framework for understanding the process of passing from this life into the next, something that was here and now, and based, if not on what hardcore scientists would call "science," at least on unbiased observations.

Another thing that happened was an experience that my father had. My dad was the head of psychiatry at a hospital in a city where there was also a medical school. He served as an associate professor in psychiatry at the medical school, where he participated on the committees of psychiatry residents. Just as a note of explanation, when a person goes through medical school, and after they've received their MD degree, they go through a residency program in their chosen specialty, where they are supervised by a group of faculty who are called their "committee." One of the things they did at this particular medical school with their residents was to videotape sessions with a patient, and then review the tape. The committee would sit down with the resident and critique the session. My dad happened to be sitting in on one of these reviews where the resident was working with a patient who'd had an NDE. None of the other people in the review were aware of NDEs, but my dad had "read the book" so to speak, and could explain the phenomenon to the others in the room. The thing that made this incident really significant for me was that, according to my dad, the patient knew things as a result of his NDE that he could not have known through natural means. The patient was aware of what was going on with his family members who were miles away, when he was clinically dead in the hospital. His family didn't react well to that – they told him he was crazy, hence the session with the psychiatry resident.

Personal Experience

One thing that came out of this introduction to NDEs was a fascination with the concept of a "life-changing experience." Dr. Moody had described the NDE as generally being a life-changing experience for those who had experienced it. Somehow they were fundamentally different than they had been before. They were the same people as before all right, but they no longer had any fear of death. They were more patient and loving with those around them. They had a profound sense of purpose. I would say that they had gained a profound spiritual quality. I am still as fascinated by this concept of the "life-changing experience" as I was when I first learned about it.

The problem with reading about all this stuff is that it is, at best, second-hand information. It's all someone else's experiences, not mine. How can I really understand it and accept it at a fundamental level without experiencing it for myself? My dad, a psychiatrist, always asked the question of how do you describe the taste of a banana to someone who's never eaten one? I yearned to have an NDE for myself, so that I could know. I wanted to taste the banana for myself.

Well, I didn't have an NDE. What I had instead was what I call a "Rememberance" – I remembered in a dream the dying moments of my previous life. I was in the tailgunner position of a bomber, what I believe was a B-17 or something very like it -- not a B24 or B25. The configuration of the tailgunner position in a B-17 appears to match what I remember in terms of seating, gun placement and windshield, while the other bombers I've seen with a tailgunner position are configured differently. During the dying moments, I was hit by machine-gun fire from a pursuing fighter plane. I can't describe to you the horror of the moment, but what also came through in the emotions was a strong sense of amazement of why would one human being be so driven to do this to another.

I might think "well, that was only a dream," except for two things. I don't often remember dreams, even the day after I've had them, and I've never had a dream that was as vivid and with such strong emotional content as this one, before or since. There wasn't anything strange or "twilight zone" about this dream like there is with others. It was just like remembering what I did an hour ago – if I did something I knew I was going to need to remember later. Some of the details have faded over the 25 or so years since I had the Rememberance, but then much of the other details of my current life since that time have faded as well, even more so.

Another interesting thing about this experience is that I later came to realize I'd been having a child's version of this dream recurring all during my childhood.

When I was growing up through pre-school and elementary school years, my family had a station wagon that we would travel in when we all went together. There were seven of us – my parents, brother, three sisters, and myself. Since I was youngest, I "got" to ride in the rearward-facing jump seat in the very back of the station wagon along with my next older sister. The recurring dream I'd had during my childhood was that I was riding in the back of the station wagon, and there was a lion chasing the car. I had this dream at least 4 or 5 times, and each time I was terrified of the lion during the dream. When I awoke, even at an early age, I didn't understand the terror because I

Rules of the Spirit

knew that the rear windshield would have protected me from the lion. I didn't understand why it would have been so terrifying.

Sometime after having the Rememberance, I realized that the earlier, recurring dream was the same dream as the Rememberance, but put into symbols that were meaningful to a toddler. The backseat of the car represented the tailgunner position, while the lion represented the fighter plane. In the real incident, the plastic windshield and structure of the aircraft did not offer effective protection against the fighter's machine guns, and that was the root of the terror.

So, I didn't get the NDE, and probably just as well – the saying goes "be careful what you pray for." I didn't remember the time in between lives, but I definitely have a first-hand understanding that there's more to life than what happens between the birth and death of a single earthly life. There's more to it than meets the eye, so to speak.

Thus began my *real* spiritual journey.

I sometimes wonder what influence it would have had on my parents if they'd understood that by having me sit in that rear seat they were placing me in a situation that would trigger remembering the horrific dying moments of my previous life. What changes would an understanding of carrying past-life issues into the current life, coupled with the use of meridian tapping techniques like Emotional Freedom Technique, have made in my life? On the other hand, I've learned to value the challenges I've faced, even when they weren't much fun. We'll explore that attitude in Chapter 9 – I find it a milestone indicator for people's spiritual journey: whether or not they consider painful experiences to be a blessing.

Chapter 3
A New Paradigm for Living

"The best proof of love is trust."
— Joyce Brothers

World Vs Spirit

I mentioned in Chapter 1 the fascination with the phrase "We are IN the world, not OF the world." That phrase suggests a dichotomy, a paradox in our living. If we are IN the world, but not OF the world, where ARE we of, and how does that affect and influence who we are and how we live?

My answer, as I've said, to "where ARE we of" is Spirit. We are of the Spirit. I've also heard the phrase "We are Spirits having a Human experience, not Humans having a Spiritual experience." So, that's great. We are of the Spirit. So what? What does that mean; what is its significance? What does that say about our reality?

The source of Spirit is God, so that means we are of God. We are the Children of God, many Christians would say, although they would also almost in the same breath deny their inheritance. For instance, modern Christians don't really believe that "miraculous" healings can take place. If I demonstrate such a miraculous healing by helping someone get rid of their headache using Reiki, they would instantly label it as "of Satan" and freak out about it in fear. What is it with modern religion that teaches if you don't understand it, it must be feared? After all, Jesus himself said "Greater things than these will you do," referring to his own miracles. Especially how is it that Religion teaches to fear? Spirituality has nothing to do with fear, as we'll explore later in this chapter.

If we are Children of God, that means we would be imbued with the qualities of God. Genesis 1:26 says "Let us make humankind in our image, according to our likeness…" Does that mean God has ten fingers and ten toes? I think not – it's the Creative Spirit of God that we inherited. If we are to fully live our inheritance as Children of God, it seems appropriate that we should live the qualities of God. These form what I believe are the truth to our reality, the "Rules" to live by.

Love

Let's start our exploration by asking what is God? Some would say that God is Love. If we use that as the primary quality, then Love becomes the primary "Rule" that applies to us as Spirit. What works for Spirit life is built on a foundation of Love. Many of the "Ten Commandments" embody that truth. Jesus said "'Love the Lord your God with all your heart and with all your soul and with all your mind.' This is the first and greatest commandment. And the second is like it: 'Love your neighbor as yourself'. All the Law and the Prophets hang on these two commandments." (Matt 22:37). Love is the most basic characteristic of our spiritual nature.

What does Love mean? Modern English has come to use the word as being the same as an extreme level of "liking" something. If you look up the word love in the dictionary, you'll find any number of definitions, both noun and verb, that have nothing to do with Love – and likely none that do define Love. Someone might exclaim "Oh, I love that sweater," but that's not Love, that's something called "cathecting." Many people mistake Love for the feeling of emotional attachment to a person or thing, but I promise you emotion has nothing to do with Love. People talk about "falling in love" or romantic love. I promise also that isn't love, it's a chemical trick our bodies play on us. It feels really good in the moment, and causes pain when we do something or something happens that threatens that relationship, but it has nothing to do with Love. Love isn't something you *feel*. And it's not something you do for emotional reasons.

The word Love is a *verb* – it's something you *do*, not something you *feel*. It seems to me that I could live my life consistently acting out Love without ever experiencing the *feeling* most people associate with Love. For instance, as I pass through a day in my life, there are countless ways I can be loving to those around me, through holding a door, or complimenting something. I don't have an emotional attachment to that person; I know nothing about them except what I can sense in the moment! I may feel good about doing whatever act I've chosen to do, but that's more a question of being satisfied that I am meeting my self-appointed goal of being a Loving person.

Love can be acted out by simply smiling at someone. Dr. Paul Ekman found through research that not only does the face reveal the emotions a person is feeling, because emotions trigger certain of 43 different facial muscles to act, but by intentionally using those muscles the person may experience the emotion tied to the expression. It's also well known that people tend to "mirror" facial expressions; for instance if I smile at someone, they are likely to smile back. When they smile back, they will feel the emotion of happiness behind the smiling. They will feel better. So just smiling at people in everyday situations can be a very simple act of love because it helps and encourages them to feel better.

Scott Peck, MD described Love as "the willingness to improve one's self for the benefit of another." I would define it as "the act of seeking and doing that which seems to serve the highest good." Keep in mind that as a human it's very difficult to discern the "highest good." It can take a lot of hard thought and soul-searching. Also, keep in mind that we're not talking about pleasing the other person – sometimes what serves the highest good can be unpleasant, which gives rise to the term "tough Love."

Grace

I would say that the next most important quality of Spirit is Grace. What is Grace: what does the word Grace mean? Grace means to me the "living out of Love." It means responding to every situation in a way that reflects the Highest Good, as I understand it. It means unconditional Love – that no matter what happens, the Love has always been there and will always be there. The relationship and the caring cannot be destroyed, no matter what happens, no matter how spectacular our mistakes.

The Worldly concept of "quid pro quo" or "this for that" has no meaning in the presence of Grace. It has no meaning in the reality of Spirit. Grace means "this, because it's the Loving thing to do, the act that serves the Highest Good." The "this for that" concept is what I call "transactional" mindset. Grace has no concept of a transaction or contract – Grace works in terms of Covenants. A Covenant is a one-sided agreement where one party agrees to do something for another, with no requirement or expectation from the second party. Anytime you see something that follows the "this for that" mindset, you can be assured that it is a worldly thing, not Spirit based. "This for That" is a scarcity mindset concept, something we'll explore in

Chapter 7. Basically scarcity mindset is saying that I have to maintain balance, because if I give without expecting return I will become depleted – my needs will not be met. But scarcity is a worldly concept. Spirit lives Abundance, which says that whatever I need will be automatically created for me – out of the unlimitedness of Spirit energy! So Spirit does not need to seek compensation. Spirit is free to demonstrate Grace.

One of the things I was taught in my Reiki classes is not to use my own energy in a treatment. For one thing, my energy is not appropriate for the person receiving the treatment. But the main thing is that by using my own energy I am depleting it. The proper way is to channel the energy from Spirit, which is limitless and wholeness. This is how Abundance works: receiving from Spirit whatever is needed.

The dictionary definition of Grace is "the free and unmerited favor of God." In other words, I don't need to *do anything* to receive the gifts of Spirit. I believe that gives a pretty good idea of Grace. Grace is serving the highest good, in all situations, regardless of the past or the future (remember time has no meaning in Spirit).

Trust

Finally, the third quality is Trust. Trust means that I know you will do the best you can in any situation – and that's the truth of it: that we all do the best we can in the moment, all things considered. Spiritual based trust takes that into account; it doesn't depend on the other person agreeing to the Spiritual ruleset. True Trust is just as unconditional as true Love. Trust says that I'm going to accept you and love you no matter what your choices are: unconditional love. This is the basis of Covenant – the one-sided promise. God trusts us to do the best we can. I believe that's part of why you don't see obvious "divine intervention" on a regular basis. This is also a large part of the lesson that Jesus teaches us in his willingness to be sacrificed. By being willing to be sacrificed, he demonstrated trust in God, that life isn't the all-in-all, that as a spirit he was safe and nothing truly harmful – in a spiritual sense – could possibly happen to him.

Imagine a parent that doesn't trust their child in anything, but rather pushes them out of the way to do whatever needs to be done in every activity. This isn't particularly healthy. Where is the opportunity for the child to learn and grow on their own? They will remain a helpless child as long as they are not given the opportunity to experience things for themselves, to make a few mistakes and learn from the experience for themselves. I've said that the role of a parent is to work themselves out of a job. In order for a child to become a healthy, happy adult, they must be given opportunities to learn, and to experience the result of that learning. They won't be able to do that if the parent is hovering over them, doing everything for them, and preventing them from doing anything for themselves because they "might break it" or "might get hurt."

Now, imagine an environment where it is impossible for the "child" to be damaged in any way – the ultimate "sandbox." They are surrounded by loving "elders" and are given access to whatever knowledge they seek, and can do whatever they want without fear. They can experience pain or pleasure. They can create whatever they want. The role of the "elders" is to assist and encourage, but only assistance and encouragement as is asked for by the "child." They can throw sand, and observe the consequences. It is a learning, creating experience, but there is nothing to fear, no permanent negative results. It's all creating, and experiencing, and creating further based on the experience. This is how I perceive the mortal existence. The things we get so wrapped up about really have little significance in the spiritual sense. It's all good!

Fear

Now that we've explored the Spirit side, let's look at the other side of this dichotomy: the World. The World in most ways is the opposite or diametrically opposed to the ways of the Spirit. Take the first quality of Spirit: Love. There are many opinions about what is the opposite of Love. The one that seems to best fit this paradigm is that the opposite of Love is FEAR. The Worldly way is the way of Fear. Because we've "bought into" (or been indoctrinated into) the ways of the world, we live in Fear, and we live out of Fear, meaning that much of our behavior is built on a foundation of Fear. Anger is always built on a foundation of fear. Scarcity mindset is based in fear. The prevalence of fear in our experience is part of the inheritance from Adam and Eve, but we'll discuss that in Chapter 7.

I believe babies do not experience fear when they are newborn. They are not born in fear. They definitely have likes and dislikes in the moment, which they will let you know about in no uncertain terms. They also may have a natural reaction to a certain stimulus such as falling. But they don't have fear. They learn to fear. Fear is not natural to them. They have to learn fear, because fear is a worldly thing, and they've just come fresh from Spirit which has no concept of fear. You can see this play out in a kitten who also seems to have no fear and will 'attack' a large dog.

Fear drives out intelligence. When you slip into fear, you are unable to use the intelligence you have to make rational decisions, so a decision you make in fear, if you could call it a decision, is much less likely to serve your own good, and even less the highest good. Fear is really good at getting you to jump – sometimes, but the jump is just as likely to be from the frying pan into the fire. Fear is also just as likely to cause you to freeze. The decision to jump or to freeze is not a measured decision. Fear is not very good at getting us to a better place. I'll talk about that more in Chapter 6.

An environment of Fear leads us to try to fulfill our own needs and desires rather than looking to the highest good. We learn to use Fear as a means of getting what we want. Because we live in Fear, we feel the need to control our environment. We must control our circumstances as well as the people around us, because if we don't, our fears will become realized. Control becomes the second rule of the World. One must Control, in order to deal with or avoid the Fear.

Control & Power

The opposite of Grace is Power. Grace means "Willingly, free and unmerited, because it's the right thing to do." Power says "because I'm stronger than you and I can make you." Negotiation is a form of exercising power. If you can find out what I really want or what my other circumstances are, you can leverage that knowledge to gain power over me and get a better deal for yourself, at my expense. You fill the need to address your scarcity by creating more scarcity for me. You could say that I freely agreed to the transaction, when my agreement is under duress.

The opposite of Trust is Control. If you don't trust someone to do something you want them to do, then you are going to feel a need to Control them. If you don't trust circumstances to provide what you need, then you're going to feel a need to Control your circumstances rather than letting it happen in the natural flow of things. This for That is a form of controlling another – getting someone else to do what you want.

The challenge here is that we are all fearing something, we're all attempting to Control our circumstances, and as long as we're living in and out of Fear, our needs, wants, and fears often conflict. The Controlling becomes a Power play between individuals or groups of individuals. If what I want and what you want conflict, then we get into an ante-up race of who can control the other.

The one who has the most Power in the circumstance wins, the other loses. Whoever has the most Power gets what they want. It's always a win-lose situation; he who has the most Power wins. The concept of Win-Lose is a very basic Worldly concept that has no meaning in the Spiritual realm – the Spirit knows only Win-Win and Lose-Lose. There is a saying that "Power corrupts, and absolute power corrupts absolutely." This corruption is because Power becomes the final blow to our connection to our Spiritual reality – it's what pushes us over the edge into the insanity of the Material or Worldly mindset, so the more Powerful we become in the worldly sense, the more our connection with who we really are is broken. When we are disconnected with who we are, we are living in unreality: we are spiritually insane.

Rules in a Nutshell

So, here are the Rules in a nutshell, in the form of a diagram for the paradigm. The Rules of the World are listed on the left, and the Rules of the Spirit are on the right. I often refer to the Rules of the World as "Control-Power-Fear."

Paul McKinley

World	Spirit
Fear	Love
Power	Grace
Control	Trust

An interesting, and I think really crucial, observation that I've had about the Rules paradigm is that the Rules of the World only *seem* to work, while the Rules of the Spirit actually do work, *always*. I believe this is because the Spirit is the reality, while the World is the illusion, the dream-world, the insanity.

If you think about it, you'll realize this is true. You may be able to get what you want from someone through intimidation (Fear), but the result will always be at least somewhat unpredictable and may not be what you wanted at all. The beaten dog may slink away, but it may also turn around and tear your throat out. Fear only has the appearance of working. I mentioned earlier about fear driving away intelligence, so it's not surprising that a response gained from creating fear will tend to be unpredictable. Fear is also a "Fight or Flight" type thing, so if what you're trying to achieve doesn't fit those two responses, the response is not likely to be what you want.

It's been well understood over the ages that people will do things for Love that they would not do for Fear. Love is often the motivator that leads individuals to overcome their fear and do things that we marvel at as heroic, even to the point of death. This is borne out in scripture: "Perfect Love casts out all Fear" and "Greater love has no one than this, than to lay down one's life for his friends." Love is more powerful than Fear. My observation is that way of Love – the way of Spirit – always works. It is the real Reality. It is the Truth. If I can train myself out of the Worldly indoctrination, and live totally by Love, Grace, and Trust, I will always receive what I need, my relationships will be healthy, and I will enjoy life to its fullest.

Our willingness to do things out of Love that overpowers Fear is Truth, but it is also our spiritual heritage, like inheriting crooked toes or blue eyes from our parents.

I find that by understanding this paradigm, it helps me to recognize Worldly habits and actions, both in myself and others. I'm not responsible for the way others behave, of course, but as I identify the Worldly habits and actions in myself, I can begin to act on them, and replace them with acts based in Spirit. As I really begin to understand how to act in the Truth of the likeness of Spirit, I then begin to improve my own life. As I become more Spiritual, I am happier, and those around me are happier. They also notice the difference, and some are challenged to work on adopting the same mindshare and behaviors in their own lives.

Chapter 4
The Reality Inversion: Forgiveness and Apology

*"For every minute you remain angry,
you give up sixty seconds of peace of mind."*
— Ralph Waldo Emerson

Forgiveness and Apology

Another interesting phenomenon that this paradigm helps us to understand is that the Rules of the World twist spiritual concepts or Truths to be the exact opposite to what they truly are; this is what I call a "Reality Inversion." It's not that reality is really inverted, but rather that our perception of reality is upside-down or backwards.

I remember reading about an experiment that was performed using special goggles that invert the visual image so that for the wearer of the goggles everything appeared to be upside-down. During the first four days nothing remarkable happened. The images seemed inverted, and as soon as the goggles were removed everything was right again. On the fifth day, however, the images appeared upright again when the goggles were being worn. Taking the goggles off resulted in the images being inverted again. The brain had adapted to the inversion and taken the inverted image as now "normal." In much the same way, we have taken as "normal" the "inverted" perception that the Worldly mindset presents.

Paul McKinley

Forgiveness and Apology is one of the best examples of this "Reality Inversion." Our whole concept of the purpose and function of forgiveness and apology is inverted. For instance, if I do something that harms you, the World says I "owe" you an apology, and you may or may not "forgive" me for this event, holding the Forgiveness over my head as something I must earn. This is actually the exact opposite of the truth: Forgiveness is for the Forgiver, and Apology is for the Apologetic.

Does this seem strange to you? Let's examine this concept. Take for example a psychopathic criminal. Does it do the psychopath any good to forgive them for their crime? They are likely not mentally capable of recognizing what they've done, or even that they have or have not been forgiven. What effect does it have on them whether they are forgiven? Nothing! They don't care, nor are they capable of understanding it: it has no effect on them whatsoever. Does withholding Forgiveness undo the crime? Even if they were sorry for their deed, would it change the reality of the harm done? It would not. This is true for the mentally competent as well: does giving or withholding Forgiveness change what is or erase the harm? Of course not!

On the other hand, look at the effect on the person who has suffered the harm. By harboring the bitterness, hurt, anger and hatred towards the criminal, they only bring themselves additional harm. Do you really enjoy being bitter or angry? Some people do, but that's their own neurosis/psychosis. Ask your physician what effect hard emotions have on your health and you'll probably get an earful: high blood pressure, autoimmune diseases, maybe even cancer. I believe it was Buddha who said "Refusing to forgive is like drinking a poison and expecting the other person to die." That's one of my favorite quotes; for me it is right up there with Ralph Waldo Emerson.

Rules of the Spirit

Let's look at a special case: when the one you need to forgive is someone who deeply and genuinely cares about you and regrets what has happened. Refusing to forgive in this situation is not only abusive to yourself due to the harm of the held negative emotions, but it is creating harm for the other person. Through unforgiveness, you are yourself becoming the transgressor. Carried to an extreme, you may even destroy the relationship with that person. I have news for you; if you destroy the relationships with the people who care deeply about you, you will live a very unhappy life! You will have harmed yourself to an extreme!

Do you enjoy being around people who are bitter or angry? You may understand why they're bitter, but it doesn't make it pleasant. Often people who are acting out of bitterness bring themselves more bitterness by alienating those around them, and leading people around them to do things in a way that is, shall we say, less than optimal. It's a vicious cycle: bitterness and negative emotion just breeds bitterness and negative emotion in those around us, as well as creating situations that bring us more bitterness and negativity. Bitterness and negativity attracts more bitterness and negativity – on more than one level, as we'll explore in Chapter 8

Where's the sense in withholding Forgiveness when it only harms yourself? This is why Jesus counseled Peter to forgive "even seventy times seven." By the way, "seventy times seven" in this context does not mean 490 times or even "a great many times." The symbology of the numbers means something like "until the forgiveness is perfect and whole" or in more modern language "whatever it takes."

Paul McKinley

Forgiveness

Let's examine forgiveness itself. What does it mean to forgive? In its most basic sense forgiving means letting go of the negative emotions associated with an event. Is it easy? Well, at first maybe not, although I think that as you grow spiritually and exercise that "forgive" muscle, it becomes easier in time. As people become more adept with the Law of Attraction, they become more cognizant of where their emotions are going, and they learn to let the negative emotions go faster and without as much drama.

I mentioned forgiveness is associated with an event. It's actually not the event, but rather your *perception* of the event. The need to forgive is triggered by negative emotion, and the negative emotion is triggered by an event, but it's really our perception that the event is "bad" that results in the negative emotion. But this is a judgement, and we have control over our judgement. Events in and of themselves are not good or bad, as we'll explore more in Chapter 9. It's really more a question of whether you like or dislike whatever it is – whether you enjoy it or not. Just as an example, you might say that pain is bad. OK, I understand that you may not enjoy pain. However, pain can be associated with things that you might judge to be good, such as the pain that results from exercise that you're not used to doing. As the avid exercise people say: "no pain, no gain." Another example might be lancing a boil – it's not much fun during the process, but the alternative is a maybe lower grade but much longer term pain, or even a boil that continues to get worse. So yes, you may not enjoy it much at the time, but your perception of the event is that it is "good." Would you feel unforgiving towards someone who had lanced a boil for you? I'm reminded of the Chicago song "If She Would Have Been Faithful" where the song describes a person who realizes that the "wrong" a past partner did resulted in something much better in their life.

The challenge in forgiving is the perception of "bad"ness in the moment. It's hard to let go of that. The fact is that forgiving is a *conscious* decision, a deliberate act, at least at first until it becomes habit. And of course the more energy you put into the event and the negative emotion, the more the event and emotion gets bigger, so sometimes it takes re-deciding, and re-deciding, and re-deciding. That's part of what Jesus was referring to with the "whatever it takes" thing: you just have to keep at it, to keep deciding to let the negative emotions go, until there's no longer any negative emotion associated with the event. You just have to keep deciding it's not worth it, it's not hurting anyone besides yourself, and let it go. Again.

Finally, as I'll describe more in Chapter 9, it helps to understand that all things and all events are good. "Count it all Joy, my brothers, when you meet trials of various kinds, for you know that the testing of your faith produces steadfastness." (James 1:2-3 ESV) When you begin to perceive all things as good, even when you don't enjoy it much in the moment, it changes the whole character of your perception of things and events around you. I would go as far as to say you may get to the point where you no longer feel the need to forgive because you no longer feel the negative emotions related to events that aren't very enjoyable. You can get to the point where your focus is on the mystical anticipation of the good you know will result, without knowing what it will be in the moment. The negative emotion just doesn't come up. It isn't there.

Forgive & Forget – the Misconception

Now, don't get me wrong on Forgiveness. A common phrase is "forgive and forget." I do not support the concept of forgetting the incident, but rather that the forgiver would do best to totally and completely release any negative emotional content attached to the event. The point here is that the event itself is part of your experience: it's part of who you are at this point. There are gifts to be had, lessons to be learned, spiritual growth to be gained in any and every incident, regardless of whether we enjoy them at the time or not. Honor your experience! Really forgetting an incident would lead to allowing ourselves to be violated in the same ways again and again – and this isn't healthy either. It would also mean failing to learn from the incident. Often I learn things for myself by observing the "mistakes" others make. I'd much rather learn by others' mistakes than having to experience it for myself! But even more so I want to learn by my own mistakes – after all, I paid for the knowledge with the experience! Tying forgetfulness with forgiveness would interfere with that learning.

Tying forgetfulness with forgiveness also presents an impossible task. It's an impossible task for a healthy person to truly forget anything. Hypnotists have proven that even small details can be dredged from someone's memory through the use of hypnotism. And even without that, you can find yourself being reminded of things long forgotten by something that happens or something you see in the moment.

There's also the concept of being careful what you pray for. My mother was a strong believer in just forgetting things. If there was anything she didn't like, or didn't want to think about, she just decided that she would forget about it. Her solution to things she didn't like was to forget. Eventually she developed Alzheimer's or similar dementia, which started out with just simply not being able to remember things. Do the two go together? Did the insistence on forgetting actively result in the dementia? No one will ever know for sure, but I have noticed that diseases are often symbolic of the way we live and think. Spouse Ann and I have been aware of the relationship between emotions and diseases. I knew of one person whom I had identified as being, as I called it, "shaking in his boots" from constant fear. Nobody else really identified him as being fearful, but it was obvious to me. This person ended up contracting brain cancer and died from his cancer. We looked up brain cancer and, you guessed it, the underlying emotion was fear.

There is biblical reference to God forgetting our sins in Isaiah 43:25: "Remember your sins no more." However, there is another verse earlier in Isaiah 1:18 that says "Though your sins are like scarlet, they shall be white as snow." The point here is that it isn't that the "sin" itself is forgotten, just that it is not remembered as sin. The negativity associated with it is resolved and dissolved. I believe God simply doesn't remember them as transgressions but rather as situations we put ourselves in or through, which become opportunities to grow.

The Higher Good would be better served by coming to recognize the blessings that have resulted from the event and learning to be thankful for the event. This won't necessarily happen overnight. Many times it's taken me years to recognize the blessings that have come from an event. My current philosophy is to recognize that the blessings are there even though they may not be immediately obvious. Isn't that the "seventy times seven" perfection of releasing the negative emotion: to become thankful for the blessings brought by the event?

Apology

The flip side of Forgiveness is Apology. What is Apology? It is the acknowledgement of our own action and responsibility in an event. What role does it play? The fact is that we cannot control our own behavior unless we can recognize what we are doing and take ownership of it. It's not uncommon these days to see one person harm another, and then blame any scapegoat imaginable, up to and including the person they've harmed. Western society has a widespread psychosis of seeking to blame first rather than look within. It's always someone else's or something else's fault, never our own. My own country, the United States, is particularly bad about this, which leads it to be the most litigious (lawsuit-happy) society in the world. This attitude is illustrated in the cartoon character Bart Simpson's common phrase "I didn't do it" which he pops out any time he feels attention is moving in his direction.

By abdicating responsibility for our actions and refusing to look within, we cripple ourselves. We can really only control ourselves, we are really only responsible for ourselves. If we refuse to look to, and live out of, our selves (note the distinction "our *selves*"), well that's just insane. It places impossible expectations on ourselves and others – a recipe for failure. Conscious living requires introspection. It means considering my actions and their potential outcomes, so that I don't carelessly harm those around me.

The fact is that whether or not you take responsibility for your deed, you still suffer from it yourself. If you're always carelessly stepping on other people's toes, you may wonder why people are avoiding you or are treating you poorly. If you are habitually careless about how your actions affect others, like the cartoon character Bart Simpson, it will always be you that people suspect. Only when you recognize what you are doing can you begin to observe yourself and work on changing your behavior. This is the real role of Apology: to really take ownership of your own actions, so that you can begin to change your behavior and grow spiritually – to reclaim your spiritual inheritance by learning to act out of Love.

Do you ever "owe" someone an apology? No! Well, maybe I should qualify that. The only one that you "owe" an apology to is yourself. Mind you, you may actually be apologizing to someone else, but the benefit of the apology falls to you, not them, so you owe it to yourself, not them. You owe it to yourself to apologize, because only through apologizing do you really internalize ownership and responsibility for whatever has happened. Only through ownership can you begin to change.

It may be that you cannot actually apologize to the other person: they may have passed on, or they may be too upset with you or otherwise passed out of your reach. That doesn't matter. You don't own their situation or emotions. Just do the apology! Write them a letter, even if you burn it afterwards. Go look in the mirror and apologize to them – because you're really apologizing for yourself. Just do it! Remember that it's through your acknowledging your part in the event that the benefit comes. Until you do, you're carrying around that baggage, and it will weigh on you until you let it go.

Spiritual Rules applied to Forgiveness and Apology

Let's look at Forgiveness/Apology from another perspective. If I've done something to harm you and I truly give a hoot about whether you forgive me or not, that indicates that I care about the relationship and have already taken ownership of the deed. Withholding forgiveness in this case is reduced to a power-play: it is a way of manipulating someone who's made a poor choice or had an accident. It's a "Control-Power-Fear" thing, rooted in the World, disconnected from Spirit.

If you think about it, it's really a bit of cruelty. Let's say I did something that harmed you, but I've acknowledged my part though apology, and done the best I can to make it good, recognizing that some harms cannot be put right. At that point, holding the grudge is just rubbing my nose in it. I've done the best I can, there's nothing else I can do. It's just a question of your holding on to the hurtness, and then using that hurtness as a justification for your own aggression. Now you are the aggressor. This is not healthy. It's not healthy for me, it's not healthy for you, and it's destructive to the relationship.

An enlightened understanding of being forgiven is that I might desire your forgiveness, not for my sake but because I understand the effect that lack of Forgiveness has on you. My wish for forgiveness is not about wanting to be forgiven myself; it is vested in my wish for your wellbeing, and has nothing to do with me. This is an attitude based in Love – seeking always the Highest Good. For example, once when Ann was working one-on-one with a colleague they had an argument about a project she was responsible for. The colleague stormed out of the room slamming the door. Ann then made herself available throughout the day, deliberately working close to him because she knew he needed to apologize, and he did before the end of the day. She had already forgiven him but she knew he needed to come clean on his side for him to feel better.

Self-Forgiveness

Self-forgiveness is probably the most important aspect of forgiveness. One of the important things that people need to understand is that, if you can't forgive someone else, you also cannot forgive yourself. Because after all, we've all made mistakes, we've all done things we wish we hadn't. If we find it difficult to forgive others, then we know that at some point there's the difficulty in forgiving ourselves. Christians are familiar with the Lord's Prayer, which includes the phrase: "Forgive us our debts, as we forgive our debtors." The typical focus is "Forgive US our debts" but the second part is more important: "as we forgive our debtors." Somewhere down in your conscious or subconscious mind you know that if you're not forgiving others, basically the prayer is saying "I don't forgive others, so don't forgive me either." My deservingness of forgiveness is based on whether I forgive, so if I don't forgive others I'm saying I cannot be forgiven. That's really tough to see yourself as undeserving of forgiveness. There's no way out of that rathole!

Forgiving ourselves is just as important as forgiving someone else. If refusing to forgive is like taking a poison and expecting the other person to get sick, what about when YOU are the other person yourself? That's the only way that the poison is effective! It's guaranteed to cause problems! All sorts of illnesses result from lack of self-forgiveness. It's easy to push down the thoughts of self-forgiveness, to put it off or to avoid confronting the self-forgiveness issue, but the issue remains and it affects the things you see showing up. The lack of forgiveness is eating away at you every minute of every day. It's destroying your health, it's causing you to react to situations in ways that aren't beneficial to you, in ways that do not serve the highest good. So, Self-forgiveness is just as important as forgiving someone else.

Self-forgiveness can often be more difficult than forgiving someone else. Why is that? For one thing you may tend to deny that you've done something that needs forgiveness. Another reason is that you probably hold yourself to a higher standard than others. The fact of the matter is that you are human, and just as subject to making mistakes as anyone else. We are all the same in that way. Holding yourself to the higher standard where mistakes are not acceptable means that when you do make mistakes, those mistakes become figurative rocks in your knapsack that you have to carry with you wherever you go, weighing you down, distorting your posture and sapping your strength. The only solution is to learn to be loving of yourself, and to forgive yourself – as you forgive others.

Paul McKinley

Judas Story

The Judas story is a good example of lack of self-forgiveness. One of the messages that I've given many times is the "other side" of the Judas story. I call it "The Saddest Story in the Bible" or "The Hardest One to Forgive." It's a good message for the Sunday after Easter.

It's common knowledge in Christian tradition that Judas was the one who betrayed Jesus. Judas is the one that everyone loves to hate. But there's another side to this story. There was a sect in Jesus' time called Zealots, who believed that the Messiah would be a military leader who would free the Hebrew people from Roman rule. Judas was not described as a zealot, but one of the other disciples was. Let's assume for the moment that Judas was of like mind to the Zealots. He clearly believed that Jesus was the Messiah – he'd been accompanying Jesus for several years. He'd heard the wisdom, seen the miracles. He probably thought he was going to be one of the patriarchs of twelve new tribes of Israel. He was ready for the challenge! But then Jesus started talking crazy stuff about going away! Mary anointed Jesus with nard, an expensive perfume used to dress people who have died. I'm sure the symbolism was not lost on Judas.

So, Judas decides he's going to take matters into his own hands by forcing Jesus to take action. He goes and works out a deal with the leadership to hand Jesus over to them, thinking that would force Jesus to "start the revolution." But then things don't go quite according to plan. Instead of coming out fighting, Jesus heals the guard that Peter had injured, and goes away peacefully. He then allows himself to be tortured, and killed. Judas, thinking that he's caused Jesus' murder, kills himself. This is the part I refer to as being "the saddest story in the Bible." If you understand the story from this context, you begin to understand just a little bit of the anguish that Judas must have felt. From the point where he tries to return the money, his world comes crashing down on him and there's nothing he can do about it. Jesus himself said "It would be better for him if he had not been born." I don't believe that was condemnation but rather empathy for how he knew Judas would feel after the fact.

The thing to remember about this story is that Jesus had already forgiven Judas, even telling him "do it now." What Judas did had to be done according to prophesy, and who knows how things would have turned out otherwise. Only through the crucifixion and resurrection could Jesus have demonstrated his mastery, to show us that we need not fear death, that we could endure even an agonizing death at the hands of others and still be willing to forgive. How different the story might have been, had Judas been able to forgive himself and had not killed himself? How would it have been, had Judas been there when Jesus appeared in the Upper Room? Jesus invited doubting Thomas to put his finger in the wound in Jesus' side; would he also have assured Judas of his forgiveness and explained to the others how Judas had played a part that nobody would have wanted to play?

Chapter 5
The Half-Truth

"The most dangerous untruths are truths moderately distorted."
— Georg Christoph Lichtenberg

A Spoonful of Sugar

Another interesting observation that comes out of the Rules paradigm has to do with Truth. One might expect that the Spiritual realm would be characterized by Truth; there's no surprise here.

The assumption, however, might be that the World would be characterized not by Truth, but by lack of truth. There would be no surprise there either, except that's not been my observation. On the contrary, what I've noticed is that the way of the World is not lack of Truth but rather what I call the Half-Truth. And, more often than not, the Half-Truth results in the Reality Inversion I mentioned earlier. It's a very curious and interesting phenomenon.

I think the reason the World deals in Half-Truths (rather than pure untruth) is because people generally recognize things that are blatantly false. If I tell you something that is patently untrue, you would reject what I'd told you straightaway. But if I couch the lie as a portion of a greater truth, it's not so clear anymore. The 1960's film "Mary Poppins" popularized the song "A Spoonful of Sugar Makes the Medicine Go Down." And so it is with Truth for our minds clouded by the Worldly insanity:

a spoonful of Truth makes the UnTruth go down. In the most delightful way, if you'll pardon my ironic continuation of the lyric.

And down it goes quite well. It's not Falseness if it contains the Truth, is it? You're walking along just fine down the path of truth, and suddenly you're not in Truth anymore. Except that oftentimes, if not most of the time, you don't notice that you've veered off the path. I'm reminded of a scene in Tolkien's "Lord of the Rings" series where the band of dwarves strayed off the elven path through Mirkwood by becoming enchanted by mysterious lights. Once off the path they can't find their way back and are only saved by being captured by the elves. So is it with the half-truth; you become enchanted by the parts that are truth, and once off the path you don't even really recognize that you're lost.

One thing I've also noticed is that, once people have bought into or as I say "imbibed" the Half-Truth, they will defend it to the death. After all, if I admit that I've swallowed a Half-Truth, I'm also admitting that I've been duped, that I'm stupid and foolish and can't tell the truth from untruth. I'm admitting that I've done something wrong, and this puts me out of Control, which is a Bad Place To Be in a World characterized by Control-Power-Fear. Not good! This must be avoided at all costs! I think maybe the way to produce the most vigorous defensive effort from a person or group of people is to arrange for their half-truth to be challenged.

Airpark example

I'll provide a real-life example. Ann and I developed a residential airpark community in the 1990's. A residential airpark is an airport that has residential living areas provided – homes for pilots. The residential airpark that we developed was expressly residential with no commercial facilities. I had lived at an airpark that happened by accident – a builder had developed property adjacent to a small private airport, and several pilots ended up buying houses that were built backing up to the runway at the airport. I was impressed with the sense of community at that airpark, even though it had happened by accident. The pilot neighbors, at least, all knew each other and were friends. We did things together, we enjoyed each other's company, and of course what could be better than all the trading off of airplane stories. Pilots tend to be quite passionate about flying!

When we moved to a new city, I wasn't able to find a property at a similar airpark. There were airparks around, but they were all sold out. So, I figured it was time to build another one. Part of my intent was to have the airport living where flying was as convenient as walking into the backyard and climbing into my airplane. But a big part of my reason for building an airpark was to create the community of like-minded people, similar to where I had lived before.

Unfortunately (or fortunately if you consider the "Challenges as Blessings" milestone attitude) we sold a lot to a family who lived very solidly in the Worldly, Power-grabbing mentality, which of course meant grabbing for Power in the community by trying to wrest it away from the developer – me – using that ever-powerful tool of fear. They did everything they could to convince any new residents that I the developer was to be feared, that I was going to take advantage of them and do things that would be harmful to them, that I was generally an all-around bad guy.

Because we were also living in the community, this family became our neighbors. One day as I was working in the backyard, a member of this family drove by and waved. My arms were full, so I couldn't wave back, but what the neighbor told the other community members was that I would not wave back, as if I was snubbing this person. The Truth is that, no, I didn't wave back. But that's only half of the truth. By neglecting to include the little detail about my arms being full, the neighbor was only telling the part of the truth that suited his needs, which slanted it in a way that sounded bad, that made me out to be the one who was being un-neighborly and unfriendly, and helped to turn the other neighbors sentiments negatively. There were plenty of other examples of how the Truth was twisted by this family, but the end result is that it alienated the other neighbors from me as well as each other, and created an adversarial environment in the community, not just with us the developers but between all the neighbors.

It didn't matter what I said, or how carefully I tried to explain the truth; like the Jonestown victims the neighbors had already "drunk the cool-aid" so to speak. It didn't matter that anyone with half a wit would recognize that the shenanigans that this neighbor claimed I was up to would be total counter to my interests. It would destroy my ability to sell lots in the community, not to mention destroy the whole purpose I was trying to accomplish in the community, which was to create a real Community of people with a strong common interest, people who depended on each other, people who enjoyed each other, did fun things together, and truly cared for each other. It would harm me much more than it would any of the neighbors. If any of the neighbors had really thought about it in an honest way, without the injection of unfounded Fear, it would have been blatantly obvious to them.

Thankfully, there was one family who were spiritually advanced enough that they saw through the garbage, and behaved in a sane way throughout the ordeal. They not only helped to inject – at great odds – a little sanity into the neighborhood, but became for Ann and me a bit of the "light in the darkness." Through their level-headedness, they helped me to make fewer mistakes than I might have otherwise.

Sadly, in doing what appeared to be serving themselves by grabbing for Power in the community, these neighbors destroyed both for themselves and for the whole community the greater good of the Community that I was trying to build. We'll explore this more in Chapter 7 Scarcity Mindset. They didn't understand the greater good that I had planned. The worldly mindset blinded them to the greater good. That's really sad, especially because they will never understand what they could have had except that they destroyed it.

Instead of having a neighborhood of friends who could depend on each other and really enjoy life together, the environment degraded to the lowest common denominator of, you guessed it: Control-Power-Fear. The whole neighborhood devolved into everyone being angry and hateful with each other. Yes, they were friendly amongst themselves at times, but generally everybody trusted nobody. Everyone had seen how their neighbors could behave in matters that pertained to the neighborhood, and even though they had "drunk the cool-aid" they had also been introduced to the dark side of all their neighbors, and at some level found that disturbing.

Ironically, the power-grabbing family moved away sometime after we had moved away. They destroyed the community, and then walked away.

Half-truth in Forgiveness and Apology

Let's look at the Half-Truth as it applies to the Forgiveness/Apology Reality Inversion. Both the World and the Spirit say that Forgiveness and Apology are valuable, even crucial. As I've mentioned, the Reality of Spirit is that the benefit of Forgiveness goes to the Forgiver, and Apology benefits the Apologist. That's the Truth, and it's based in Love, a characteristic of the Spirit. By switching or "inverting" the supposed beneficiaries, the World makes the Forgiveness/Apology into a Control-Power-Fear thing. That little switch, the little half-truth of who benefits, corrupts the whole understanding. The truth part of it is that Forgiveness is needed, and Apology is needed. Both are important. The untruth part of it is buried down in the fine print where it defines who are the beneficiaries.

Conveniently the corruption works in a way that plays into the hand of control-power-fear. Instead of forgiving for my own benefit – no power to control someone else there – I can hold the forgiveness over your head to get you to do something I want or otherwise control you. I can even beat you over the head with it by making sure you never forget how you've harmed me, reusing over and over the same possibly trivial error to exercise my power. There's no telling how long I can keep up this control I have over you by refusing to forgive. Keep in mind that this only works because basically everyone alive has bought into the Worldly mindset and the Worldly concept of Forgiveness and Apology, so they believe that they need something from you: your forgiveness.

Let's take the Forgiveness/Apology thing a bit further. I have observed that if a person can't forgive others, they can't forgive themselves either. We've all done things we aren't proud of. We've all done things that harm either ourselves or others. I believe that even extremely narcissistic people understand at some level that they have done things that were harmful to others.

Rules of the Spirit

Whenever you find yourself unwilling to forgive another, at some point deep down, maybe so deep it's at the unconscious level, you're saying to yourself "if they don't deserve forgiveness for that deed, then how does my deed compare? At what point does a deed become 'forgivable' or 'not forgivable'?"

And so not only does the poison of negative emotion, resulting from refusing to forgive another, fester within you, it adds to all the negative things you've done in your own life. The venom you hold for others adds to the venom you hold for yourself. Things get pretty toxic. Eventually the toxins result in disease: cancer, arthritis (an auto-immune disease, basically self-destructive) or whatever. Is it clear how unforgiveness only hurts yourself?

Half-truth in politics: give 'em what they want

Political figures are full of half-truths. They will promise all sorts of things that they think people want in order to get elected. Some of the things they promise actually sound good, but you have to dig further to get to the truth. Affordable health care becomes the rallying cry, but the way it gets implemented forces people into buying health insurance, and the health insurance rates become so expensive that many if not most of the people who had been buying health insurance previously can no longer afford it because the price has tripled in a few short years. The only people who really benefit from the plan are people who are broke and qualify for government-provided insurance, and the health insurance companies. I remember one of the promises made during the rallying for the Affordable Care Act: "You can keep your current doctor, you can keep your current policy." The truth was that most of the existing policies did not comply with ACA and so the insurance companies discontinued them on the half-truth that they were noncompliant when the real truth was that the existing policies were cheaper and therefore less profitable. The insurance companies are also phasing out the "PPO" style policies in favor of HMOs – which severely limit your access to the doctor you want.

I have a friend who lives full-time in an RV – a travel trailer. She'd been finding work that took her to different places around the country for one to several years at a time. But her insurance policy was cancelled because it was not ACA compliant. All she was being able to find at that point were HMO-style plans, but the HMO plans for Texas, her declared state of permanent residency, did not provide for medical care in other states where she was working. Her only choice was to move back to Texas. That seems to me quite a restriction on freedom, in a country where we pride ourselves on freedom.

I'm also reminded of Bill Clinton's statement when his oval office sex-capades broke in the news. He stated "I did not have sex with that woman." The truth was that he did have a sexual encounter with someone other than his wife, in the Oval Office – the highest office in the country. The half-truth part comes in when you use a very narrow definition of what constitutes sex. The amazing thing to me is that people nowadays no longer remember that incident: it has hardly affected Bill Clinton's "brand" at all. If anything it has only served to elevate his brand as being slick.

Finally there was the Richard Nixon scandal with Watergate, wherein he claimed "I'm not a crook." Again the truth is that there were some very serious wrongs committed. The half-truth is when a very narrow interpretation of what is a crime (crooked) and what is an innocent mistake. Eventually Nixon did pay the price, and since his running mate had already resigned and been replaced by Gerald Ford through Nixon's nomination and congressional confirmation, our country had its first non-elected President. By the way, the 25th amendment defined how the succession would take place, and that amendment had conveniently been passed just a few years earlier in 1967.

Parents: empty promises, idle threats

I so often hear people defending child discipline through physical violence such as spanking or whipping with a belt. The half-truth here is that, yes, it may get them to stop the unwanted behavior. Or, it may not. The challenge comes in situations where a child is neglected. In such a case the spanking may be the only way to get attention, and it's no longer a punishment – it's no longer a means of negative reinforcement. I remember a situation with a little girl whose mother had decided that discipline was a bad thing, and so held herself to the standard of providing no discipline. My opinion is that discipline is critical to child development; it's just that there are loving ways to provide discipline, and violent ways of providing it. Anyway, the mother would ignore the child's misbehavior, and ignore it, and ignore it, until she just couldn't stand it anymore, at which time she would "blow up" with an angry fit, spank the girl and confine the girl to her room. The challenge was that the more the child would misbehave, the more the parent would withdraw into her own conflict of contradiction. The more the parent withdrew, the more the child would misbehave so that they could get some attention, even if it wasn't very loving. After all, some attention is better than none. The other part of it was that some days mommy feels good, and the boundary is far and very flexible. Other days mommy isn't feeling so good and has a short temper, so the boundary is close and inflexible. But from the child's point of view, she never knew where the boundary would be *this time.* I am reminded of the Skinner experiments where he discovered that he got a stronger behavioral response from pigeons with a random, intermittent reward than if he used a consistent, more frequent reward. So mommy's random response produced a much stronger impetus for the child to act out. It's like turning the crank on a jack-in-the-box: you know the thing is going to pop out and startle you, but you just have to keep turning the crank in nervous anticipation. The child became so obsessed with finding out when mommy would blow up - *this time* – that she couldn't play normally. The end game of behavior that started out as a dysfunctional way to get attention devolved into simply a means of manipulation for the child. I know of another child who got all the attention he wanted. When he was confronted with a jack-in-the-box that popped out, he then wanted nothing to do with the toy, even after it had been put away for a year and re-introduced.

Another example is the parent who makes idle threats to their child as an attempted means of behavior modification. The half-truth here is that the parent is making the threat thinking they will follow through, but then the truth is that they do not have the discipline themselves to follow through. This is also a good illustration of how the Rules of the World in general don't work. So the parent makes a threat to the child, trying to change behavior. The child pushes the boundary, as all children do; this is a natural and healthy exploration of their world. But the parent doesn't follow through on the threat: the child gets away scot-free! Wow, that's interesting! Let's try that again! The more this goes on, the more the threats escalate, and the more the child gets away with it until the child is totally out of control and the parent, thinking that they've been loving to the child, is left wondering what happened. I will tell you that lack of discipline is not being loving to a child. The discipline does not have to be violent, but it does need to be *consistent*! I knew of one parent who threatened her children with ripping their arm out and beating them over the head with it, and at the top of her lungs. The household was filled with screaming idle threats, and of course the children would ignore the threats. The parent had to practically manipulate the child like a puppet to get them to do anything. The children also learned to be manipulative, using, for example, false claims that an adult had harmed them, in an effort to disarm the adult. The lesson here is that the parent is trying to use Control-Power-Fear as a means of disciplining their children. It doesn't work, unless your goal is to produce adults who are quite adept at the Control-Power-Fear thing rather than having spiritual skills that will actually serve them in adulthood.

Poverty as a spiritual directive

A good example of half-truths in some Christian and possibly other traditions is the concept that poverty is a good way of becoming spiritual. I would agree that it is a good thing to be not so married to your possessions that you lose sight of your spiritual connection. That's the truth part of this idea. But it doesn't help you spiritually to be poor. One of the challenges of being poor is that your mental activity is always going to be focused on providing for yourself – how are you going to get the bills paid, how are you going to be able to afford the food you need, how are you going to pay the rent? The everyday process of paying bills is bringing you negative emotions. Your emotions are not going to be positive about your financial situation, and by the Law of Attraction, you will attract to yourself more unpleasantness about your finances.

On the other hand, think about what happens if you are wealthy. What can you do with the wealth that you have? Wealthy people can and often do use the power of their wealth to contribute to the benefit of many people. As an example, William A Cooke Foundation in Virginia was founded by a wealthy real estate investor. He formed a non-profit foundation to manage his investments and arranged things so that, when he passed on, his foundation would provide benefits to others, such as scholarships for college students and grants that would benefit the community. Now, his foundation continues to buy and sell real estate, provide rental properties, and private investor funding for other investors as well. All of the profits from these activities are used for good cause. All this could not have been done if Mr. Cooke had stayed in poverty for "spiritual" reasons.

Raymond Aaron himself reminded me that Jesus' group of disciples had a treasurer. His comment was that "broke people don't have a treasurer." There are a couple passages that people use to justify the poverty idea. One is the instance where Jesus told Peter to go look in the mouth of the first fish he caught. This was a lesson for Peter – and us – to trust that our needs will be met, and also that we can create that which we need. Do you think that coin just happened to be in the mouth of the fish? The other is the story of the rich young prince, who Jesus told "If you want to be perfect, give away your riches and follow me" whereupon the fellow went away sadly. The point here was not that he had to give away his riches to be spiritual but rather that the prince was so married to his possessions that he felt they were more important than his spiritual development. Money was his master, rather than he being the master of his money. You cannot serve two masters.

Chapter 6
The Insanity of Fear

"Fear defeats more people than any other one thing in the world."
— Ralph Waldo Emerson

The Daneel Story

One of the challenges of the Fear thing is that when someone goes into fear, whatever intelligence they may have presumed to have goes out the window. I'll describe a cat I once had, named Daneel, as an example. When Ann and I met, she had two cats: Callie, a patch calico; and Barney, a black and white. I had four cats; Pete, a solid white cat; Groucho, a patch white and tiger stripe; Giscard, a black and white; and Daneel. Daneel was a beautiful long-hair gray cat. Everyone who saw him commented how beautiful he was. Unfortunately Daneel epitomized our observation that long-hair cats used too much protein for making fur and not enough protein for making brains. Daneel, for all his beauty, wasn't the sharpest knife in the drawer. Mind you, I'm a "cat person" and not prone like some people to think that all cats are dumb. That's just not true, cats are different than dogs; they have different motivations. Ann's cat Callie seemed to have the intelligence of a 3 or 4 year old child – at times you could "see" the gears turning in her head.

Lack of wit wasn't Daneel's greatest challenge, however; it was that he had no control of his fear. The slightest thing would set him off, and when he snapped into fear, whatever small intelligence he had disappeared in an instant. In his haste to get away from whatever had startled him he would smack into legs or furniture or whatever: he was totally mindless at that point. Similarly Ann had a story about a kitten whose fear had caused it to run underneath the very lawn mower that had sparked the fear.

Fear can prevent communication and learning for people as well. I have noticed that if a conversation pushes someone into fear, that person no longer hears what is being said in the conversation. They become so focused on their fear that they can't comprehend anything that is being said: they hear the words but the content is just babble. The wise speaker recognizes that this is happening and can back off and find a way to help the listener recover from the fear, after which a different course of discussion can be used to get the ideas across. This is why a doctor will always ask that you bring someone with you when they have bad news to relate. They know that in your fear, you will not hear anything.

Clearly fear can be an unhealthy thing if it causes us to do things without thinking about them. We've already discussed how the neighbors in the community destroyed their opportunity to live in a healthy, harmonious environment by allowing themselves to be manipulated into fear by the half-truths being told by the power-grabbing neighbors. Fear may push me out of my rut, but the chances that I will improve the situation through fear-based action are not very good. I'll take even poorly thought-out plans of action over fear-based any day, thank you.

Ann's Panic Attacks

Not too long after our son was born, Ann fell prey to panic attacks. Panic attacks are a form of irrational fear that can be brought on by trigger events or even just recurrent thought patterns. Ann's first attack was brought on by a discussion about exactly that: panic attacks. Ann is quite empathetic and found herself connecting very deeply with the emotional stress that was being described by the presenter leading the discussion. I don't think it was strictly the empathetic connection; I believe she had some unresolved insecurity that set the stage, maybe past life issues. At any rate, she began to feel a bit queasy and constricted, and so she left the room to go sit outside and get some fresh air. The next thing she knew she was laying on the ground, with one of the medical doctors in the group hovering over her. She had passed out from the panic attack! Someone took her home and made sure she was resting peacefully until I could return from the separate event I was attending with our son. She was "washed out" exhausted for several days after that – the event really drained her energy.

Over the course of the next few years she continued to have panic attacks, although none that caused her to pass out. Even so, she lived with the fear that she would have another pass-out episode, especially in a public place, and doubly especially while she was responsible for caring for our son who was a toddler at the time. This is a bit of a self-fulfilling prophesy in that the fear of having a fear-based panic attack keeps the panic attack ever near. One of her triggers was the aisles, people, and large enclosed spaces of grocery and other stores like Walmart. Since I was working at the time, part of her responsibility was to care for our son, so she would have to take him with her when she went to the grocery store or wherever. The thought of having him with her when she had an attack in such a public place and not being able to care for him just served to increase the fear factor for her. The panic attacks, and the fear resulting from the panic attacks, became quite debilitating for her. You can see that fear was beginning to rule her life. It was irrational fear, meaning that there wasn't anything truly there for her to fear except, in Winston Churchill's words, "fear itself!"

Fortunately Ann was able to use her intellect and her connection to spirit, along with an acupressure technique called Emotional Freedom Technique (EFT) to resolve the panic attacks. About the same time as she was having the panic attacks, she was having increasing allergy issues. At one point she was having debilitating allergy and asthma symptoms about 9 months out of the year, and she was using an inhaler for the asthma. But the inhaler had its own issues, one of which was that it was like inhaling dust, which triggered a fear of suffocating, which in turn added to the panic symptoms. Simultaneously the inhaler increased her anxiety level, which made the panic attack symptoms worse. I personally can't take epinephrine-based decongestants like pseudoephedrine because they make it difficult for me to detach from the ceiling.

Ann kept telling herself "If it can get worse and worse, why can't it get better and better?" She was introduced by a friend of ours to a Naturopathic Doctor who did allergy elimination using acupressure; a technique called NAET (Nambudripad's Allergy Elimination Technique). Ann's first treatment was for lactose intolerance – she had always been highly sensitive to milk products, and just a tablespoon of milk would send her to the bathroom in agony for hours. She couldn't eat any form of milk product, including cheese. We always thought the lactose intolerance was due to lack of ability to produce the enzymes needed to digest the lactose. Clearly it isn't, because the one treatment eliminated her lactose intolerance, *permanently*. It took her awhile to get up the courage to really test it out; after all if it didn't work the penalty was pretty severe. But try she did and discovered that she could drink milk, and eat ice cream with no ill effect! Cheese still gave her a bit of gas, but she had it re-treated and eliminated that issue. We were so impressed with the results that over the course of 9 months or so she kept going back to get more allergies eliminated, 2 or 3 at a time. One day she was treated for grasses, and for a day afterwards said it felt like bubbles were popping in her sinuses. After that she no longer had asthma. To this day she has not had any asthma symptoms. Any time she would have other allergy symptoms, she'd scurry down to the ND and have them eliminated. I also had some treatments for allergies: fungus, house dust, and jalapeños, each of which would make me sick to my stomach. I also am no longer sensitive to these things. I use jalapeños as a preventative and cure for cold and flu viruses: "a jalapeño a day keeps the doctor away!" It helps to visualize the viruses shriveling and dying as they're covered with the capsaicin, the spicy ingredient in hot peppers.

The NAET worked so well for Ann that she started researching that and other energy methods online, and came across Gary Craig's EFT site, emofree.com. She ordered his tapes and materials, taught herself the EFT techniques, and started working on herself for the panic attacks. Over a period of a year or so she resolved the panic attacks. Not only that, but prior to her EFT work, she could not bring herself to call someone she didn't know on the phone – another aspect of fear. She probably isn't going to take a job as a telephone salesperson, but calling a stranger doesn't keep her from doing what she needs to do. She's a whole new person for having conquered her fears, and I am so proud of her for it!

Attracting the greatest fears: Barney & the Snake

One of the challenges of fear is that because it is a strong emotion, it tends to create a strong activation of the Law of

Paul McKinley

Attraction. I'll discuss the Law of Attraction in Chapter 8. So, that which you fear, you are attracting to yourself. The more you fear it, the stronger the attraction.

    I mentioned earlier that when Ann and I met, she had a black-and-white cat named Barney. Barney was a very sweet cat, a bit clumsy but normally very easy-going. But Barney had a fear of snakes. He would freak out at anything that looked like a snake, like a string on the floor, a belt on the bed, a tie on a chair or whatever. When we moved into the country to build the airport community he became even more fearful of snakes, which was probably a good thing since there were rattlesnakes around in that area. One day we found a rattlesnake that I had run over with the tractor/mower – apparently the snake had struck at the bottom of the motor because it was chopped into sausage-link pieces. Anyway, Barney was so fearful of the snakes that he attracted one. We had a tenant in a rental property that disappeared, leaving most of their stuff behind, including a 30" pet snake in an aquarium. We had to clean out the apartment to rent it to the next tenant, but we also had to keep all the possessions while we tried to track down the previous tenant to return their belongings. This meant of course that we had to care for this snake, for about 2 months. Barney couldn't believe we'd bring a snake into the house; he really flipped out. We weren't enjoying it much either – it took up room in our crammed house, and we had to feed it a live mouse every week or so. Since we weren't very good at catching mice in the field at that point, it meant having to go buy a mouse, to feed this snake that didn't belong to us. The point here, though, is that Barney attracted to himself the very thing that he feared most. We eventually had to sell all of the tenant's belongings, but the snake was the hardest to sell. When we finally sold the snake, you guessed it; the tenant finally contacted us to get their stuff. We did save their family photos and shipped those back to them.

Anger based on fear

One of the things that I've noticed is that anger is always based on fear. This is actually a fairly useful observation, because if you can identify the fear that the anger is based on and address that fear, then you can effectively dissolve the anger. Please notice that anger being fear-based places it squarely in the realm of worldly Control-Power-Fear. Remember that the worldly rules only appear to work, but don't really because the results are unpredictable. Anger does have the ability to goad us into taking action where otherwise we might not, but the action taken is likely to have unintended consequences. Anger, and especially rage, can break down your social barriers to the point that you begin to do things that will result in harming others or yourself. When your anger or rage results in your not caring about the outcome, it's likely that things will follow that will have consequences you will not enjoy. It may also be that your anger engenders fear in people you care about, causing them to withdraw, or it even destroys that relationship. It may be that you do things that get you into trouble, or hurt people, or things that you regret.

4 year old killed by road-rage in Albuquerque

A good example of the destructive nature of anger is a road-rage based incident in Albuquerque that occurred as I was finishing up this book. One driver fired a gun into another car, hitting and killing a 4-year-old girl. Apparently the whole incident started out with the suspect driving in an unsafe manner, with gestures and retaliatory driving to follow. Apparently within the space of two miles it escalated to the point that the suspect pulled out a gun and started firing, hitting the girl in the head. This is a very sad incident.

My speculation is that the suspect lived a life of anger. Apparently he had numerous brushes with the law, but had somehow managed to escape prosecution. Based on that I'm also guessing that he was a Stage One Chaotic, as I'll discuss in Chapter 10. Through his own careless and likely anger and fear-based actions, he sparked the fear in the victim, who also acted out through anger – based on fear – and things escalated to the point that an innocent girl was killed.

It seems likely that the outcome of a moment's rage for the suspect will be pretty harsh. The whole incident sparked the horror of the entire Albuquerque community, so my expectation is that this person has lost his freedom probably for the rest of his life; in other words the life he could have had is forfeit. It's my understanding that people who have committed crimes against children have a very rough time in prison.

Fear as a chemical addiction

You may wonder about people who continually do things that are fearful, such as base jumping, or watching scary movies, and so forth. What happens is that when the fear emotion is stimulated, a whole range of chemicals are released in the body, including serotonin and dopamine. Apparently dopamine can stimulate both the fear and pleasure sensations, depending on where in the brain the chemical is applied. I think that's probably why there can be a thrill associated with fear activities, which may or may not seem desirable depending on the person. It would seem that if dopamine is being produced in the brain, it would tend to spread to other parts of the brain. Depending on a person's physiology, they may have more or less of the pleasure stimulation to go along with the fear. If enough of the pleasure is stimulated in an individual, it could cause them to become addicted to the chemical pleasure that results from fearful situations. So a fear-addicted person might tend to go

Rules of the Spirit

for more and more intense fearful activities in order to achieve the chemical high. Hopefully they also apply some intelligence in how they go about the activities in order to stay reasonably safe; otherwise I would expect them to live a relatively short life once they've become addicted. There's a saying in aviation circles: "There's old pilots, and there's bold pilots, but there's no old, bold pilots."

Chapter 7
Scarcity Mindset: The Fall from Eden

"People in distress will sometimes prefer a problem that is familiar to a solution that is not."
— Neil Postman

Adam and Eve: Half Truth strikes again!

I would expect that Jewish, Christian, and Muslim traditions would be familiar with the story of Adam and Eve. They started out in a paradise called Eden, where all their needs were met. They didn't wear any clothes, because they didn't feel the need for them. They had all the food they could want and pretty much did whatever they want. The story goes that there was one tree whose fruit they should not eat: the tree of knowledge of good and evil. Adam and Eve had no concept of "Good" and "Evil" initially. Everything was good! But God had told them to steer clear of the knowledge of Good and Evil tree "or you shall surely die." But then "the serpent," interpreted by many as Satan, sold them on the idea of eating the fruit, and all sorts of bad things happened as a result, including getting kicked out of paradise.

I happen to believe that this story is not literal, but as so many of the stories in Biblical text are, it is allegorical, which means it tells a story to illustrate a point. Pretty much all of Jesus' teachings were in the form of allegory, with only a couple times that he, in exasperation at his disciples, explained the story point-blank because they were being too dense to understand the allegory. Anyway, I believe the Adam and Eve story is allegory, and maybe the most important story in the Bible because the mindset described by the allegory has such a powerful and challenging effect on mankind today.

So let's start off with the bit about the Tree of Knowledge of Good and Evil. It says that God said something to the effect that if Adam and Eve ate of it, they would surely die. Those of us who know the story know that they didn't die, at least not physically. This is an example of a Half-Truth, although it's not clear to me where the half-truth originates. I'm not prepared to say that God told the Half-Truth, because God is quintessential Spirit, characterized by Truth. Maybe the Half-Truth originates in mankind's misinterpretation, or maybe it was the serpent who phrased it in such a way. The serpent is symbolic of the Worldly mindset, of the dark side of our ego; so it would be in character for the serpent to twist the truth into a Half-Truth. It's interesting to "watch" the interaction of the serpent and Eve. He doesn't come out and say "that's not true" but rather quizzes Eve on the particulars first. Eve herself elaborates on what was originally commanded, adding her own bits of half-truth. The serpent also uses another powerful Half-Truth in his sales job, saying that the fruit would give them knowledge of good and evil (true) which would make them like God (not true – they were *already* made in God's image).

So Eve ate some of the fruit, and handed it to Adam to eat also. Although they didn't physically die, the innocent, trusting, uninhibited, satisfied persons that they were before ceased to exist. They no longer saw themselves as perfect, seeking to cover themselves. They were ashamed of themselves, seeking to hide from God. They now experienced fear where they had never experienced fear before.

Here's the point. The fruit wasn't literally something to eat: it was a *concept* – the concept of *good and evil*. We've all heard the phrase "you are what you eat." There are cultures that believe if you eat the brain of another creature, you will gain the knowledge that other creature had. So it's a very strong symbol to be "eating the fruit" of knowledge – or concept – of good and evil. Prior to imbibing that concept, humankind knew only good. Prior to taking in that idea, humankind knew only *abundance*. Prior to this point, *only good and abundance existed!* Evil and scarcity didn't exist, because mankind had not yet created it with the idea! This concept became the archetypical challenge for humanity, the single most important pitfall that is in my opinion the root of all the challenges mankind faces, and we've been struggling with it ever since. This is the real meaning of the story of Adam and Eve. This is the crux of the Fall from Eden.

Fall from Eden: Scarcity and Abundance cannot coexist

Although the Biblical narrative doesn't talk about it, Scarcity and Abundance are part and parcel with the Good and Evil concept. Let's examine Scarcity and Abundance just a bit. What does Abundance mean? It means that whatever I need or want gets created out of nothing – or out of limitless Spirit energy if you will. Because it's created out of no-thing, it means that there will always be enough to meet my needs. My needs will always be taken care of: I do not need to worry about that. Spirit is able to create what is needed out of no-thing, so it doesn't matter what is in front of us, it doesn't matter what is needed. Not only are my needs met, but I can freely give of what I have because I know it will be replenished. There's no need to hold back. "Give and it will be given to you, a good measure, pressed down, shaken together and running over." (Luke 6:38 NIV) If our true nature is Spirit, and Spirit creates what it needs out of nothingness, Abundance is our spiritual truth.

Paul McKinley

What does Scarcity mean? It means that everything is limited, that no new thing is created. It means there's no guarantee that my needs will be met; in fact I may have to take away from you in order to meet my needs. Scarcity breeds greed. Scarcity breeds selfishness. Scarcity breeds violence, because if I believe I must take away from you to get what I need, and you believe you must defend what you have, we're going to do battle at some point when we each try to use our worldly control-power-fear to meet our needs. Scarcity means I will live in fear; fear that my needs will not be met, fear of you because I believe you will be trying to meet your needs at my expense, fear of the world because I know bad things happen in the world that will take away from what I need.

Adam and Eve lived in Abundance prior to the fall. They had all the food they could eat. They didn't have the idea that they needed clothes; although it says when they did they sewed together fig leaves. I have heard that fig leaves are pretty rough and scratchy, so it would seem that there is some symbolism there as well. The knowledge of nakedness really just means they had also taken on another false idea of shame or low self-esteem. The rough and scratchiness of their solution is symbolic of the chafing that this idea of shame creates, and the solution is simple: lose the shame and low self-esteem, lose the cover-up, and the chafing goes away. Anyway, as long as Adam and Eve had only the idea of what they needed being abundantly available to them, the Law of Attraction made it happen for them. The challenge comes when the idea of scarcity enters into the mind. Law of Attraction says that as soon as you start thinking about scarcity, then scarcity begins to manifest. As soon as you start manifesting scarcity, then it becomes your reality. You cannot have Scarcity and Abundance coexist, just as you can't have both light and darkness. So once Adam and Eve had taken on the idea of Evil, and along with it Scarcity, they could no longer live in Eden. All things became difficult for them.

We continue to struggle with this to this day. Because we have the idea of Scarcity, we create scarcity in our lives, in our environment. We've forgotten how to create what we need from nothing. Because we've forgotten how to create intentionally, we create, through the Law of Attraction, scarcity. It's like a self-fulfilling prophesy: the more we worry about scarcity, the more scarcity we create.

Scarcity mindset in our language: creating reality

Scarcity mindset is so pervasive that it has become imbedded in our very language. Many of the common idioms and clichés reflect the scarcity mindset. We don't even think about what it is that we're saying. A common one that comes to mind is "I can't afford that." This mindset is based on the idea that I can only have based on what I have already – and what I have already is limited and therefore scarce. So I'm locked into a state of "what is" rather than the unlimited possibility of "what could be." Our spiritual reality is that nothing is impossible. Masters of the Law of Attraction teach us that all we need to do is put the mindset energy into what we want, and then allow it to be created for us. We can cooperate – or not – with the process, but we don't really have to do anything to make it happen other than wait for it. So to say "I can't afford that," which really means "I can't see myself having that with the resources I have now," is denying the Law of Attraction. Or maybe I should say it's aligning with a lack of "that." That's scarcity mindset! I don't have to be able to "afford that." All I have to do is put focus and energy into the desire, allow myself to become aligned and resonate with that possibility, and it will come to pass of its own volition through pure and elegant creation.

Another scarcity mindset phrase is "you only live once." I find it interesting that people who subscribe to Christian theology will adopt this mindset, which is based on the idea that your life begins at birth and ends at death. It denies some basic Christian beliefs. Many Christians believe that life begins at birth and continues through death to infinity. My understanding and experience is that life extends from the infinite past to the infinite future. Actually time has no meaning for spirit so discussing life in this context makes no sense. "You only live once" mindset also sets the stage for pretty much anything goes, because you have to grab everything you can to make it worthwhile.

Have you heard the expression "Money doesn't grow on trees?" Actually, anyone who runs an orchard knows that money DOES grow on trees, just not in the printed form. The meaning behind the phrase is that money is hard to come by. From a worldly, scarcity mindset point of view, this can be true, but it isn't true in a Spiritual mindset or context. One time Ann was struggling a bit with the "ask and you shall receive" concept. She had some bills to pay, and needed money to pay them. So she put out the intention, through telling her "guides" that she needed money. Early the next week a check for $80 came from a credit card company saying we had paid too much interest; several days later another check, this time for $120, appeared from the same credit card company explaining that they owed us more rebate. At that point, Ann thanked her guides saying "Thank you, that was nice, but a hundred dollars here and a hundred dollars there is not going to pay the rent. I need thousands!" A few days later she saw a notice in the newspaper of unclaimed funds in the state treasury. The notice included a list of names of people who had unclaimed funds, and how to recover them. She went down the list and, lo and behold! there was my name on the list. It turned out that an error was made by the title company on a real estate transaction several years earlier, to the tune of several thousand dollars! This is how the Law of Attraction works: things get created from nothing. How would we have known about the overcharged interest on the credit card, or the underpaid rebate, or most especially the error in the real estate closing where countless eyes including our own had carefully inspected the transaction looking for errors? Money *really* does grow on trees, figuratively speaking.

And finally there's the cliché about "the rich get richer and the poor get poorer." There is some truth to that, but it acts on several levels. For one thing, poor people do not have a true mental concept of having large sums of money, and so what they create for themselves is small amounts of money. Also because they do not have wealthy habits, they tend to spend the money they have less than wisely. They do not manage their money very well. Wealthy people, on the other hand, have to an extent mastered using the Law of Attraction. They have created for themselves a concept of larger amounts of money and therefore attract to themselves larger amounts.

The challenge with these phrases and clichés that I've mentioned, and many many more that I'm sure you can think of, is that by accepting these things as true, and repeating them in our day-to-day conversations with others and especially with ourselves, we are exercising the Law of Attraction and thereby bringing them forth into our reality. Another cliché that I like because I have observed it to be quite true is "be careful what you pray for." The challenge here is that the Word (Capitalization significant) is powerful. That which we say, either aloud or just to ourselves, starts the creative process. So if you're saying something to yourself, even mindlessly, you are putting energy into creating what you are saying. Adding the "not" to the phrase doesn't help, as I'll examine in Chapter 8 – Spirit has no concept of negatives, so your subconscious doesn't hear it. Saying "Do Not Forget!" is the same as saying "Do Forget!" – so you forget!

Christmas Card Story

Here's a different way that scarcity mindset filters into and dominates our lives. When I was growing up, I received a solicitation from a Christmas-card company to sell their Christmas cards. Basically all it required was that I send them back a reply, and they would send the kit I could use to then go door-to-door and sell Christmas cards. I think I was probably in 5th or 6th grade at the time. So, I sent it off and a few weeks later received the kit. My mother noticed the kit coming in the mail of course, and we had a little talk about it. Basically she was concerned about me feeling bad about what she perceived would be predominantly negative responses. Her attitude discouraged me to the point that I didn't even bother trying to go sell the cards. Not only did I not even try, but it instilled into me the idea that I couldn't sell anything, which influenced my attitudes about what I could do, even into mid-life.

I'm reminded of the story of a classroom of girls who were challenged by their teacher to name their feature that was most beautiful. Most of the girls would say "my eyes," which is a safe bet – nobody has ugly eyes. They're all pretty much the same besides color. But when it was the little red-headed girl's turn, and she said "my eyes," the teacher said "No, your eyes are not what makes you beautiful." The girl carried with her after that the idea that her eyes were ugly, when the truth of the situation was that her eyes were great but it was her red hair that made her beautiful!

So where does scarcity mindset play into this? My mother's attitude was that the people in our neighborhood would be holding tight to their resources and not be willing to buy anything from a kid coming to the door. She was also concerned that I'd be beaten down and discouraged by that. But it turned out that she herself was the one that discouraged me, and in such a way that it influenced negatively my self-image and choices for a major period of my life. She traded the possibility of discouragement for the guarantee of discouragement. Was it true that I'd have been unsuccessful if I'd tried? We lived in a moderately affluent middle-class neighborhood, so I doubt that money would have been an issue for most of the neighbors, and the product I had was something they'd have been buying somewhere or other anyway. It's also been my experience that most people are a sucker for kids selling stuff door-to-door; I know I am. At this point we'll never know, because it just didn't happen. I was too discouraged to even try.

Let's look at how this might have played out with an abundance mindset, and a truly encouraging, loving attitude on the part of my mother. When the sales kit arrives, she thinks to herself "Wow, he's taking the initiative to do something to earn money. I need to encourage this and help him be successful. He may get some rejections, but we can deal with that when and if it comes up. He's very outgoing and will talk to anyone, so he already has some of the skills he'll need. I don't have any sales experience myself, so maybe I can find someone who can give him some tips to be more successful." Then when the time came that I might have had some rejections, the conversation could have been something like this: "Well, not everyone is going to need or want the product that you have, but that's OK. You just have to get through however many NOs to get to a YES. Keep up the good work and don't let the NOs discourage you!" Abundance mindset thinks in terms of possibilities, not drawbacks. Abundance mindset thinks not in terms of "why" or even "why not?" but rather "just do it!"

Paul McKinley

What I learned later in life is that I have – and had – a lot of qualities that could have made for a good salesperson. I am outgoing and ready to talk to anyone. I am a very good listener, able to "hear" what another person is trying to say even when they're not saying it very well. I am able to speak in a way that people can understand the ideas I'm trying to get across. This knowledge hasn't changed the things that I've done to produce income, but my attitude and self-perception has changed with the realization that this is something that I can do if I want.

Scarcity and Fear Go Together

Let's remember that fear is a worldly thing. Scarcity is also a fear-based mindset. It's based in fear, and it creates fear, because through scarcity I may not be able to provide for myself or my loved ones. The more I become afraid, the more I begin to attract things to me that are fearful. The scarcity that I attract through fear displaces the abundance that might otherwise have come to me. That creates more scarcity, and more scarcity creates more fear.

As I begin to act through a mindset of scarcity, I begin to hold in to myself the things that I have, rather than allowing things to flow. I become stingy instead of generous. Students of energy methods understand that it's important to allow the energy to flow. It's like your digestive tract. Medical professionals understand that what goes in must come out. When I try to hold things in, those around me become wary and less willing to share and cooperate. When those around me are less willing to share, because they know I'm not going to return in kind, it creates more scarcity, especially in times where I need it most.

Finally, if I fall prey to the idea that I need to take away from you in order to meet my needs, I begin to destroy relationships.

Rules of the Spirit

I begin to build distrust from my neighbors because from their perspective it looks like I'm always trying to get or take something from them – which pushes them into their scarcity fears. I may even land in jail because I've taken things that don't belong to me – that haven't come to me naturally through my abundance. When I get out of jail I find that it's harder to find a job, which creates more scarcity. It's a vicious cycle, and once you're deep in the cycle, it's very, very difficult to break out.

Scarcity's apparent benefit

You might wonder why people might go down the path of the scarcity mindset. That is, other than the fact that we tend to be taught that mindset from birth, so it's been programmed in all our lives. I think there are other reasons that support the scarcity mindset. I've already pointed out how it can get to be a vicious cycle, but I think it can also become something that enables dysfunction.

Scarcity mindset says no matter how hard I try, I will still not get what I need. So why bother? Why go to the trouble if I can never get ahead? I may as well just give up! If I do something and fail, well, I expected to fail because of my scarcity mindset, and so I got what I expected. Of course if I fail to act because I expect to fail, that is failure too so either way I get what I expected – failure.

Change the Perception, Change the Mindset

I maintain that Scarcity is the half-truth. Abundance is our spiritual truth. So how do you climb out of the abyss of the scarcity mindset that has become so habitual? How do you come to understand – I mean *really* understand – the truth of Abundance? It all boils down to perception. "You see what you want to see, and you hear what you want to hear," says the

Paul McKinley

Rockman, from Nilsson's "The Point" (1971). If you can simply accept that scarcity can be mindset rather than reality, and that through your own mindset you create your own scarcity – or abundance –you can begin to open yourself up to experiencing things in a different way.

I mentioned the process of giving up because I expect failure. That concept is a bit funny to me because it seems to me that even in giving up, I am proving that I live in abundance. If I give up, I may not be as successful as I could be, but I still have things come to me that I need. Neale Donald Walsh talked about hitting his low point, but even during that time he found the things he needed to survive. It wasn't much fun, and he didn't feel very abundant in the moment, but through the moment he received what he needed, including and especially his revelation that has helped him thrive.

I've also had my ups and downs in life – I've had jobs, I've lost jobs or quit, I've made lots of money, and I've "coasted" here and there. But I've never worried about being able to provide for myself when I've parted ways with a "job," because I've always had a deep understanding that the value in the job rested with ME and not the job. So when I left a job, I took the value *with me* to the next opportunity, where that value by its very nature begins to create new things that have value and as such provide for my needs.

My point is to choose where to place your attention, and to choose how you perceive your circumstances. Often you don't seem to have much choice in your circumstances, but you always have the ability to choose how you perceive them. Viktor Frankl didn't have much choice about being interred in a concentration camp, but he had control over his own perception and how he would respond. And so doing, he survived the concentration camp where many did not because they gave up.

Rules of the Spirit

It has been my experience that when I look for abundance in my life, I begin to see it. It can also begin to be a "vicious cycle" because as I feel more abundant, I begin to attract more abundance. The more practiced I become, the more effective I become at creating and enjoying abundance. Have fun with it! It can be a joyous thing, to keep noticing good things. And enjoying those things creates a grateful attitude, which attracts more good things to be grateful for.

Chapter 8
The Law of Attraction

"Always bear in mind that your own resolution to succeed is more important than any one thing."
— Abraham Lincoln

Introduction to the Law of Attraction

In the last chapter I talked about the vicious cycle of scarcity mindset creating more scarcity, and abundant mindset creating more abundance. This is part of something that is popularly called "The Law of Attraction." The Law of Attraction as a phrase became popularized with the video "The Secret," which came out in 2006. Basically the Law of Attraction says that whatever you put your energy into gets bigger. Some people like to phrase it in terms of vibration or frequency. Most of us have heard the term "bad vibes."

Vibration seems to be a fairly good analogy. A common example is two tuning forks that are tuned to the same frequency – if one tuning fork is struck and placed reasonably close to the other, the unstruck tuning fork will start to vibrate also. The two tuning forks resonate with each other – the energy of one is passed to the other.

I think there's probably several mechanisms for this: one would be sound waves passing through the air; another might be the vibrations passing through whatever solid objects might be touching both forks. Considering that most tuning forks are made of metal, it could be that the energy transfer occurs through electromagnetic fields. Even beyond that, there are other fields such as gravity, and weak or strong atomic fields, that could explain the resonance. I imagine that all of those forces have at least a small part to play in the transference from one tuning fork to the other.

Whatever the mechanism, the fact is that there is resonance, which is why I prefer to call it the Law of Resonance, although I'll stick to the more popular Law of Attraction in this book. It doesn't take much energy to get an object to vibrate at its resonant frequency. As a Mechanical Engineering student in college, I was shown a short film of the destruction of the bridge over the Tacoma Narrows in Washington State. Galloping Gertie as it's also known, was opened to traffic July 1st, 1940. However, the bridge was subject to up and down movement – low frequency vibration – in response to the winds passing through the Narrows. Engineering students were shown this video as an example of how aerodynamics and resonant frequency of a structure could have a drastic influence on design. In this case, the wind caused the bridge to vibrate at the resonant frequency of the bridge. When on November 7, 1940 the wind blew strong enough and long enough, the resonance increased until the bridge collapsed.

This concept of resonance applies to much more than tuning forks and bridges. It applies also to our emotions and our mindsets. Many people have had the experience where something is brought to their attention, at which point they start seeing the same thing all around them.

The Law at Work

Let's say a friend of yours buys a blue car of a certain make and model. You don't remember seeing one before, but after seeing your friend's new car, you start seeing them all the time. The phenomenon of not seeing things that are right in front of you is something that I've called "Somebody Else's Problem," in reference to Douglas Adam's "The Hitchhiker's Guide to the Galaxy." I would say that the difference is that before that time you had no resonance with that make and color of car.

Another way resonance works is through our emotions. Imagine first someone who is angry all the time. It's not difficult to see that other people will tend to resonate with that emotion and reflect anger back to that person. An angry person will attract other angry people, and the more energy they put into being angry, the better they'll resonate with one another. The interesting thing is that the angry person will see this as justification for their anger. I recently stopped for gas in Buffalo NY on the way to Toronto, in a convenience store gas station. The pump wasn't working correctly, so I had to go into the store to provide payment. The clerk, whom I presume based on her accent was an immigrant from an African country, asked where I was from and commented that I clearly wasn't from that local area – because I was courteous and pleasant with her. Clearly the norm in that particular neighborhood was for people to be angry all the time.

On the other hand, a person who is calm will tend to attract other people who are calm. Angry people don't get the "zing" from the calm person: the calm person doesn't add to their energy, or to put it another way, the calm person's energy isn't complementary to the angry person; it doesn't resonate.

Clearly our mindset, beliefs and attitudes can have a powerful influence on how we experience life. We can attract things that match our "frequency" as well as push away things that don't.

Paul McKinley

The Law of Attraction goes a little deeper than this and says that this resonance takes place at a much more profound, spiritual level, not just the superficial physical level I've just described. The Law of Attraction says that we have the ability to attract whatever it is that we want, with the limits being only one's imagination. Essentially it says that we can participate in the Creation process and "Create" whatever we want. Not only does it say that we CAN participate, but that we DO participate, whether or not we perceive or understand it. We can't choose to participate or not, we can only choose to adapt our thoughts, emotions, mindset, and actions with the understanding of this concept, and thereby choose our environment and living circumstances at a conscious level.

There are a couple challenges to this understanding. One is that when we come to fully understand the impact of the Law of Attraction, we also have to come to terms with the reality that we have created for ourselves. If we've created a reality that is unpleasant or not what we think we wanted, we also have to face the reality that it's a reality of our own choosing, if an unintentional choice. This is not easy to do, not the least of which is due to the fact that you wouldn't have been doing it in the first place if you realized you were doing it. You have to learn to recognize what it is that you're doing, when for all your life up to now it's been "Someone Else's Problem."

Integrating New Behaviors

My understanding is that we go through a process in incorporating new behavior into our habits. At first, we don't even notice our own dysfunctional behavior. At some point, our behavior is brought to our attention – either by another person, or by seeing or hearing ourselves in a mirror or on a recording. If it's brought to our attention by someone else, we'll probably go through a period of denial, until we see that mirror image or

Rules of the Spirit

hear/see the recording. We still don't recognize that we're doing it when we're doing it.

We may also do the denial of maintaining that the behavior isn't harmful or is justified. When we do that, we also have to come to recognize the harm of the behavior.

The next stage is when we recognize that we've done it, but only after the fact. It's a bit hard to change things when you don't recognize it until after the fact, but it does help to bring it home that it's actually happening. It's undeniable at this point. We see that the behavior exists, we understand the connection to an outcome that we didn't want or enjoy, but we still feel helpless to change it, because we don't recognize it until it's too late.

At some point we move into the next stage where we actually start seeing ourselves doing it *when it's happening.* I can say from my own experience this is a very "Twilight Zone" feeling. It's where you really come to terms with the existence of what some would call the "watcher" or "observer" – the part of yourself that stands to the side and comments on what's going on. Sometimes the Watcher is characterized by an "angel" or "devil" that sits on our shoulder. It's a bit like watching a movie where the character played is yourself. Like a very predictable movie, you know what's going to happen. You may be internally screaming at yourself "don't do it!" but still it plays out exactly like you know it has a thousand times before.

After a while, as you think about what happened and the negative consequences you now know are associated with the habit, you begin to get creative and think "what if I did this instead of that?" Even then, when the situation presents itself, you still do the same old thing – you continue the habitual behavior. This stage fits what the Apostle Paul was describing when he wrote "that which I know I should do I do not, and that which I know I should not do, that is what I do." But as you see yourself doing the "wrong" thing, you also start seeing yourself doing something better.

Eventually you start catching yourself in the act, and early enough to actually do something different. It may be that your new twist does not work out in reality as well as you'd planned, but I'd bet that the chances are that it turned out much better. After all, even though the behavior is new, it's based on *thought* rather than *habit*. I'll place my bets on a response that is thought out – on conscious decision – over habit any day.

One day, you start responding to the same event in such a way that the result is much better, much more in line with what you want. It may be that in the process you've come to understand at a more basic level what's going on underneath the event and have not just one good response, but a recipe for any number of good responses based on an understanding of the mechanics of the circumstance.

This is the challenge of facing the reality that we create our own reality. It takes a while to recognize it and even longer to adapt to this understanding.

Integrating the Law of Attraction

The other challenge is that, until we are confronted with the ramifications of the Law of Attraction, we have no skills or understanding of how to respond to it. How do you learn to make good use of the Law of Attraction when you've never been aware of it, and worse, you've been living the scarcity mindset that we explored in Chapter 7? It's an interesting combination of adapting your behavior, including learning to move and hold your emotions in such a state that they resonate with creating the good things that you want in your life.

Part of the challenge is that you won't really know how to make it work until you've done it… and observed the results and repeated it enough times that you *know unequivocably* that the results were in fact your own manifestation, your own Creation, your own "demonstration." This is made a bit more difficult in that usually the results don't happen right away – you have to keep up the resonance for a long enough time for the results to begin to manifest.

A good example of the time delay is the trick with the soprano who holds a high note for a long enough period that a crystal glass shatters. The glass doesn't shatter the instant the note is struck; it takes a while for the resonance to build enough energy to shatter the glass. It took hours for "Galloping Girdie," the ill-fated bridge over the Tacoma Narrows, to build up enough resonant energy from wind turbulence to destroy itself. Our own personal resonance can take months or years to build enough energy to manifest the things – whether the manifestation is intentional or not.

My father used an analogy of how do you describe the taste of a banana to someone who's never tasted a banana? I think the same thing is true with learning how to use the Law of Attraction. People who understand it can try to describe it and explain it to you, but you're not really going to "know" until you experience it for yourself. Even then I'm not sure any of us really knows it all that well, and certainly we each experience things in different ways. We stumble on things that work somewhat, but maybe the results aren't exactly what we had in mind, or it takes a very long time to manifest.

Paul McKinley

I think part of the issue is developing the ability to hold our energy, our "vibration," at a level that achieves resonance both with the Creative process as well as that which we're trying to manifest.

Some of the authors I've read suggest that you need a kind of almost childlike joyful anticipation of your manifestation. Maybe a good example would be the feeling you have when you've dropped an order for something really cool and fun into the mail. The item doesn't appear instantly, but you know it's coming, and you await with joyful excitement and anticipation. I think this may be part of what Jesus was referring to when he admonished his disciples "you must become as one of these," referring to children he was attending.

I think something like determination, knowledge that it's going to happen, trust that it's going to happen has something to do with it. I know I've manifested things over the years by a kind of "willing" it to happen. Generally for me this has been in the form of making mechanical or electrical things work, when nobody else could make it work. I made it work because I knew I could make it work. The expression of the determination is a bit like tensing up your insides; maybe that's what the Biblical phrase "girding your loins" is referring to. Except that it's not a muscular thing, it's an energy thing.

Another way I've manifested is through my ability to produce income. I mentioned previously I've had ups and downs financially through my life, but I've never become truly destitute – I've always had what I needed. I've always had a deep trust that I would receive what I needed. I never worried about being laid off or fired (I've been both), because I knew that the real value was within me, not in the job itself. Wherever I go, there also goes the value I bring; therefore I will never be without. I am always able to get what I needed, with integrity, through legitimate means.

One of my favorite quotes is of Earnest Holmes: "You will rise, and you will fall, you will get discouraged, you will get encouraged, but always you will be progressing, ALWAYS, and so you must simply stick to it and the day will come when you no longer say 'I hope, I desire, I pray,' but you will say 'I know.'" This is the way to approach The Law of Attraction. Know that it may be a struggle for awhile, but you will get better at it, and the better you get the easier it becomes.

Backyard Mountain

Ann has a couple of her own stories about manifesting. One came from her childhood. As she tells it, one day her mother told her a story about a woman who read a passage in the Bible (Matthew 17:20) "If you have faith as small as a mustard seed, you can say to this mountain, 'Move from here to there.' And it will move. This woman then prayed for a mountain she could see to move, she then looked up and the mountain was still there. The woman then exclaimed "I knew it wouldn't work." At the ripe age of 5, Ann pondered the story and looked out her back window at the flat coastal plain land they lived on and thought to herself, "A mountain would be fun in the back yard. But no, it might destroy the neighbors' houses. How about a large hill but not one that would hurt the big trees in the backyard. That is it, a small hill that us kids can run up and down on." Ann then dropped the subject and did not think about it again until years later when she was about 12, looking out the window she realized the prayer had been answered. As time passed, her father had a dumptruck load of sand delivered to the back yard, with the idea of spreading it on the lawn to help the grass. Except that he didn't get around to spreading the soil. Grass grew on the sand. So, it turned out that Ann got her mini-mountain in the backyard, without even taking further thought about it or imagining how it could happen.

Genesis, Thoughts & Emotions

The word Genesis means "the origin or coming into being of something." I think it's important to examine the process for the Law of Attraction, the Genesis of how things come about through the Law of Attraction. Basically it starts with the thought, the idea. We tend to not realize that with every thought we are creating. Much of our thoughts are fleeting, so they don't have much opportunity to resonate and as such begin to attract and create things. Thoughts that take hold and get repeated, or that are explored more in-depth, begin to create more energy and are more likely to build the energy required to begin to manifest.

Thoughts aren't the only ingredient, however. Your emotions play a very powerful part in creating. Your mind produces the idea of walking to the post office, but your feet are what put energy into that idea. Likewise your emotions are the "feet" for your creative energy. They are what puts the energy into the attraction, and the stronger the emotion, the stronger the creative force. A good example of this is the saying that "A mother's prayers are quickly answered."

Ann experienced this during her college years when her bicycle was stolen. She was going to school at Texas A&M, which has a very large campus. It was fairly difficult to get from class to class on foot if the classes were far apart on campus, also she lived in an apartment off-campus, which added to her daily travels. She was broken-hearted about losing her bicycle, and prayed for it to be returned to her. Finally she prayed that "If I don't hear back on this bicycle by the end of Friday, on Saturday I'll have to go buy a new one," with a great deal of emotion attached to the prayer. Sure enough, the police called Friday night with news that her bike had been found.

Joy is probably one of the more powerful emotions as far as creating is concerned. I find that gratefulness is a form of joy. Gratefulness is a very strong part of creating. After all, if you aren't en-Joying what you're creating, then you're not putting much energy into creating more of it.

Elegant Solutions

Drawing on my background as an engineer, I understand that there are solutions, and there are "elegant" solutions. What's the difference? I'm reminded of the old joke about the difference between a technician and an engineer: a technician will build something that will work, while an engineer will build something that *just barely* works. The "just barely" is representative of the idea that the solution will be simpler, or use less materials, or easier to manufacture. An "elegant" solution is one that has an elegant simplicity. It doesn't sacrifice quality but rather provides a quality solution that takes less effort or less energy to accomplish. One of the things I've found about the Law of Attraction is that it tends to produce what I'll call elegant solutions. The Law of Attraction works in such a way that it takes the least amount of energy to produce the result.

One of the things that teachers of The Secret counsel is to avoid being too specific about how it's going to happen. For instance, if I want a house, I could put it out there that I want a house. If you want a hill in the backyard, put it out there that you want a hill. That's a pretty easy wish. But to say I want a

Paul McKinley

house in this particular neighborhood, with 4 bedrooms, a porch, a large backyard, hardwood floors, green shutters, and a copper cupola on the roof, makes it a bit more difficult to manifest. That's not to say it can't happen that way, but it may take more time for it to happen, because more circumstances need to line up, more things need to be created, more energy to produce. That's not to say that there's not enough of all of those things; remember we live in abundance. It just limits the possibilities of how something can happen. Usually our idea of how something might happen is not nearly as elegant as the way it *could* happen when the Law is at work.

When our son Jesse was getting ready to choose a college, he was set on getting a degree in Computer Game Programming. So the wish put "out there" was for a college that had that type of curriculum. At the time there weren't very many colleges that had a Computer Game Programming curriculum. Jesse found one particular college that was an accelerated program in the Salt Lake City area, and he kind of fell in love with the place. But it was rather expensive – it would have left him with a large debt load after graduation. Their idea of financial aid was to provide a student loan. We looked at a couple other colleges, including a rather prominent college in Texas. Finally, Jesse was contacted by Champlain College in Burlington, Vermont. Champlain was the last college that we visited, and it turned out that it had the best program of all the ones we'd investigated. They put students in cross-discipline teams almost from Day One, which none of the other colleges did. They also had a program with a dedicated faculty member designed to support entrepreneurship – where other colleges talked about the percentage of students working in their field a year after college, Champlain talked also about how many of their students were working in their own businesses – that they started with the help and encouragement of Champlain College. Clearly it was head and shoulders above the rest. The best part is that, because they wanted to increase their "reach" in terms of out-of-state students and we were at the time residents in Texas, they offered a very attractive scholarship that made it the financial choice as well.

Remember that Abundance mindset says I can trust – I don't have to try to control things because I can trust, I can have faith, that my best interests are being met. Understanding the elegant solutions aspect of the Law of Attraction fits into that. I know I can just focus on the kernel of what I want, and trust that things will turn out in a way that meets or exceeds what I want. It's just up to me to guide myself into resonance with what I'm wanting to create.

When I talk about elegant solutions, I don't mean to imply that the Law of Attraction can only work in certain ways. It does not! The Law of Attraction is a spiritual thing, and as such just as easily works in the realm of what we might call miraculous. I've long said that "reality is plastic," meaning that what we perceive as reality isn't so hard and fast as we have come to believe. I've seen so many instances of ad-libbing reality that it's not surprising to me anymore. It's like we're making up our reality as we go along. It's really pretty fun when you can learn to create in this fashion; things really become limitless.

A number of years ago Ann and I were driving back to Georgetown, Texas from Glen Rose, Texas where we'd attended a church function the night before. I knew that Rev. Steve Langford, who had been a pastor at the church we were attending at the time (Round Rock First United Methodist) was assigned at Cogdell UMC in Waco, and thought it would be really cool if we could attend Sunday morning worship service with him at his new charge (charge is what Methodists call the church where a pastor is assigned by the conference). But we didn't know where Cogdell UMC was – we just knew it was in

Waco. This was before automotive GPS receivers became prevalent. Ann the Worrier was stressing the whole way driving down State Highway 144 and then 6 between Glen Rose and Waco, but I just kept telling her "Don't worry about it; when we get into the outskirts of Waco I'll go into a gas station and look it up in the phone book." So, as we come into the outskirts, I took the first exit where there was a gas station, and pulled in. As I went into the store, I thought "What the heck, I'll just ask," so I asked the clerk if she knew where Cogdell UMC was. She replied "Oh yeah, it's right across the highway here!" We couldn't see the church because of the overpass blocking the view. I've always wondered where Cogdell UMC existed before I asked that question. It's like the quantum physics problem where the location of a particle is indeterminate until the point in time that it is observed, after which its location is defined by where it was observed.

Abundance mindset does not imply lack of stewardship – it does not imply wastefulness. Stewardship simply means to cherish and care for what we have because it's through that joyful energy that we create. If we don't have any regard for the things that we create, we also lack the creative power, and our ability to create will be diminished.

Be Careful What You Pray For

You've probably heard the saying "Be careful what you pray for." That applies to the Law of Attraction, and maybe especially so. We tend to not understand that our words and thoughts are powerful. They are capable of creating things without physical effort on our part, through the Law of Attraction. The challenge is that we often, or maybe even usually, don't pay attention to what our words are saying! But your thoughts and especially words are always creating! So it is very important to learn to pay attention to what you are

Rules of the Spirit

thinking and especially pay attention to what you are *saying*. This is where that saying "Be careful what you pray for" comes from – but the crux is that whether you realize it or not *you are constantly praying through your thoughts and words.*

Ann and I are both cold-natured. When we are comfortable, everyone else is too hot. When everyone else is comfortable, we're too cold – our fingers and noses are turning blue. It turns out that our son Jesse is hot-natured. I've always said he's been a little furnace since the day he was born. Most people think of wrapping babies up in blankets to keep them warm. That was a bad idea with Jesse; he'd be sweaty and crying if we bundled him up, even when it was cold outside. We learned to feel his hands – if they were warm then so was he – and they were almost always warm. I took Jesse to an aviation-related hot-dog cookout when he was a month or two old – on a day it was 45 degrees out. One of the senior ladies at the function fussed at me about having a baby out in that cold. I told her "If he was uncomfortable, he would *let you know*!"

Because Jesse was always complaining about the Texas heat, Ann kept telling him all his life "You're going to end up in Vermont," "You're going to end up in Vermont," because in her mind's eye Vermont was an extraordinarily cold place. Think of the energy that Ann had put into that idea of "You're going to end up in Vermont," having repeated it so many times over the years. I've already mentioned that Jesse did in fact end up in Vermont, at least for his college years! He even had people native to the north fussing at him about wearing shorts and no jacket in the cold weather there! Please note how this story also underscores the elegant solution thing: the solution not only provided the "highest good" for Jesse's college wishes, but also fulfilled unwitting intent that Ann had placed for Jesse to "end up in Vermont."

Paul McKinley

Jesus: coming from the heart

Jesus talked about the importance of the things we say in Matthew 15:17-20: "Don't you see that whatever enters the mouth goes into the stomach and then out of the body? But the things that come out of a person's mouth come from the heart, and these defile them. For out of the heart come evil thoughts – murder, adultery, sexual immorality, theft, false testimony, slander. These are what defile a person, but eating with unwashed hands does not defile them." In light of what we've been discussing about our thoughts and words being powerful and powerfully creative, what do you think about some of the choice of words that people often use? I personally refrain from using what I'll call "colorful" language for that reason. It's not that I don't know the words, or their meaning; I just don't feel the need to use that kind of language, knowing that it affects the reality I create. I internally shake my head when I hear people whose speech contains an ugly word every other word. What an ugly world they must be creating for themselves! Remember that the Law of Attraction is always creating from your thoughts and words – and that emotions are what give the thoughts feet – and that your heart is the throne of your emotions. Your words come from your heart! It makes sense to pay attention to what's coming out of your mouth in words because it reflects the state of your heart. Choose your words to be uplifting! If you're making up stories about people, make it a good story, not an evil one. Find positive ways to talk about things, in order to create a positive reality that you'll enjoy. Learn to choose the words you use, because words are powerfully creative, and it makes a lot more sense to create things you choose rather than creating things out of habit that is most likely not well coupled with what you want to create.

Rules of the Spirit

Never Say Never

One of my messages, or "sermons" if you will, is titled "Never Say Never," which is a play on one of the James Bond movies. It's based on a concept that Ann and I have learned, which is that the subconscious doesn't hear the "not" in statements. This makes sense to me. It seems to me that the subconscious is our closest connection to our spiritual existence if not a reflection of spirit itself, and it makes sense that Spirit has no concept of NOT or negation.

Let's look again, for example, at the phrase "Don't forget!" The "don't" is actually two words "do not", so the real phrase is "Do not forget." But the subconscious doesn't hear the "NOT," so what it hears is "Do Forget!" or just "Forget!" Have you ever wondered why, the more someone says "don't forget," the more they forget? I'm reminded of the old saying "Why do the children put beans in their ears, when the very thing we tell them NOT to do is put beans in their ears?!" In light of this not hearing the negative concept, it seems natural that the children are going to miss the negation and do what they're being told not to do.

One time when Ann and I were in the early stages of building the airport community, we had a neighbor who had hayed their pasture, leaving standard square bales. But it rained before the hay could be picked up and put away, so despite the neighbor trying to prop bales against each other in an upside-down V so that they could air out, they mildewed. Mildewed hay is no good; it can't be used for cattle feed! So, they chucked all the hay bales over the fence! It so happened that I needed hay bales to place on our property to control erosion – mildew doesn't matter for that! – so I asked the neighbor if I could have the hay, and of course they agreed. So Ann and I went and collected as much of the hay as we could. That was BC (Before Child) so Ann had not developed much upper-body strength at the time, and so it was up to me to chuck the bales BACK over the fence, lift them up into the back of Ann's little Dodge Ram pickup truck (a Mitsubishi in Dodge clothing), drive them home, and then place them where we needed them for erosion control. I think I must have loaded that little truck up 15 feet high in the air, with bales hanging halfway out on both sides and in the back – the poor little truck was definitely loaded to capacity and beyond. And of course I had to load and stack all those bales by myself. No problem! Several months later, we were out walking down our little dirt road, and I noticed that a recent rain had displaced one of the hay bales. So, I stopped to push it back into place. Ann said "Don't hurt your back!" Guess what happened? Yep, you guessed it. Despite being able to chuck all those bales over the fence, load the truck sky-high, and then unload it again carefully placing each bale without injury, I hurt my back budging one measly bale a few inches!

Chapter 9
Right and Wrong, Good and Evil

"That old law about 'an eye for an eye' leaves everybody blind."
— Rev. Martin Luther King Jr.

The Goodness number line

I have long understood that our concept of good and bad is a matter of perception. What we believe is good or bad is based on our own concept of what it means to be "Good" or "Bad." Let's look at it this way. I think most people who've gone to school have been presented with the concept of a number line. We tend to think of a number line as being a line that extends infinitely long in either direction, and we tend to have our focus somewhere near the "zero" of the line. Here's an example of a number line:

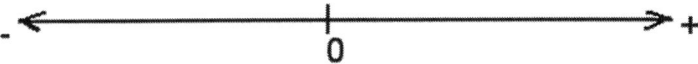

The scale doesn't matter here; what matters is the concept that there is a zero point, and the line extends endlessly in either direction, increasing one way and decreasing the other.

Now, let's superimpose "Goodness" on this line. Anything above or to the right of the zero point is "Good" and everything to the left of the zero point is "Evil" or "Bad."

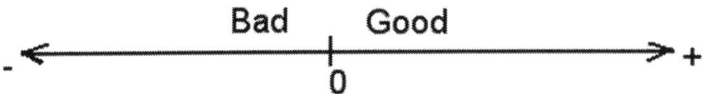

This would be a spiritual Stage Two point of view – I'll discuss the spiritual stages in Chapter 10 – that there is a well-defined demarcation between what is Good and what is Bad. No bones about it, it's either Good or Bad. Keep in mind that this is a simplification of the concept of Good and Bad, because this is a one dimensional representation of a complicated, multidimensional concept. But it provides a good way of thinking about the concept.

Goodness based on perception

The challenge is that Good and Bad are really based on perception. What one person perceives as good, another might perceive as bad. An extremist might think that killing someone that doesn't agree with them is a Good thing, where more moderate people would see killing as an unspeakable Bad. One person may think euthanasia is good under some circumstances, another may think it's bad regardless of circumstances. One person likes rain, another likes sunshine. It's all in the perspective of the individual or social group, and it's basically based on what we like or don't like. So my concept of Good and Bad becomes relative to my own personal Point of Reference. Things that I like are upscale on the Good side of my point of reference. Things I don't like are on the down side of my point of reference. I tend to judge everything based on my own perspective, which is based on my own point of reference as to what is Good and what is Bad. That point of reference can change over time as well, as I grow and evolve spiritually.

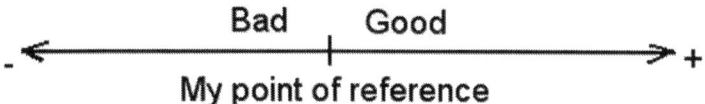

Rules of the Spirit

The point I'm making here is that there really is no definite zero point on this line. Because it's based on perspective, and everyone's perspective is different, everyone is going to "live" in a different place on this line.

Something I've noticed is that people can only discern "goodness" and "badness" a little bit upscale and downscale from their point of reference. They really only understand the concept of "good" and "bad" within a relatively small neighborhood of their own personal point of reference. This is what I call my "Frame of Reference" on this line – the space where I live and have a good "feel" for "goodness" and "badness."

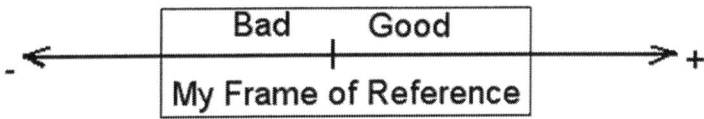

The challenge here is that our ability to perceive "Good" and "Evil" is limited to a relatively small neighborhood of "where we are." We may perceive things that are outside our Frame of Reference as being the opposite of what they are from a spiritual sense. For example, the Pharisees perceived Jesus as being Bad, because from their perspective he was assaulting the order and hierarchy they found comfortable. He threatened the circumstances and ideas that they thought were "good." But the real problem was that Jesus "lived" outside their frame of reference, and so they couldn't perceive that his presence and the things he did were "Good."

The word "sin" is commonly understood in English religious circles as meaning "breaking God's law" or to put it in a more typical and abrasive mindset "crimes against God," as if

God were vulnerable to human crimes – the concept of a "sin against God" seems a bit narcissistic to me. The word "sin" in Spanish simply means "without," "absent," or "missing." So Sin basically means something that puts distance or separation between ourselves and God – something that interferes with or reduces the connection. It doesn't hurt God, but it does create challenges in our human experience. Is it Bad? Well, that depends on the perception. I believe that all things result in good, even if we don't enjoy them much at the time, so nothing is truly Bad or Evil.

The good news is that I believe Mankind is progressing up the "Goodness" scale. The average person's point of reference is higher up the goodness scale than it was in times past, and continues to progress. Sure, there are things that happen in the current times that seem really bad. But it seems to me that if I look back in time, things were more downscale the farther back you go. 50 years ago beating a child in school was considered good. 300 years ago slavery was considered good. A few thousand years ago child sacrifice was considered good. Mankind has been evolving over time. We don't see the change because it takes many lifetimes for these types of changes to occur. We only see just the little snippet of time where we are currently living, unless we take the time to examine historical records.

Story: What good is poison ivy?

An interesting illustration of the perception of good and bad is one person's meditation on the poison ivy plant. What good is it? It can be a tenacious plant, growing up trees and other places where you might brush or grab the plant without knowing it's there, and then Ick! If you're sensitive to it, it can make you ill. When I was in the first few years of elementary school, there was a woodsy area a couple blocks from home, with a small stream running through it, and paths all over. The neighborhood kids would play in the woods, catching mussels in the stream and so forth. I remember there were a couple girls that lived across the street that got into the poison ivy, which made them ill for several days. Somehow I never had any symptoms until adulthood. When Ann and I were in the early stages of building the airport community, we tried raising angora goats for a while. We were trying to breed the natural color back into the goats; for the cottage industry that wanted naturally colored Mohair for spinning and weaving. The goats loved to eat poison ivy – and then they'd come nuzzle my arm and get the oil on me. I developed a few blisters from that, although it never was very bad.

So most people would agree that poison ivy is NOT a "good" thing. So what use is it? The story is that the person meditating on the idea came to the realization that the poison ivy was there to protect the plants around it. So, even though we may think it's bad, apparently the plants growing around it may receive some benefit. Except from goats of course.

Things to forgive based on the perception of the event

Earlier in this book I discussed the issue of forgiveness. The need for forgiveness arises as a result of an event. As I discussed, Forgiveness is the letting go of any negative emotion associated with the event. Forgiveness doesn't mean forgetting the event. It just means letting go of the "bad" feelings we have related to and associated with the event.

But the negative emotions we have about the event are based on our perception of the event. We perceive through the event that it caused us pain, or injured a loved one, or threatened our ability to satisfy our needs. We may not have had control of the situation that led up to the event, but we do have control of our perception of the event. We decide.

A good example of this is situations that arise when driving. There's lots of instances of people doing things when they're driving that may feel threatening. My perception of what they are doing can influence how I feel about the event and the person precipitating the event. I could, for instance, decide that they are a stupid and selfish driver, and be really angry at them for cutting in front of me, or nearly running me off the road. Ann has a different approach. Her initial reaction to events like that is to think that the person may have some issue going on in their life, such as being worried about a loved one in the hospital, or maybe the person is preoccupied with a difficult situation at work. There's any number of possibilities that could explain – not justify, mind you, but just explain – their behavior. Through Ann's habitual perception that there's some reason that the person needs compassion rather than condemnation, it totally changes her driving experience. The Law of Attraction kicks in at this point, so because she's not putting a lot of energy into the situation, it rarely happens to her.

The point here is that through choosing a different perception of the event, there is no negative emotion associated with it to begin with. There is nothing to forgive! It's not a withholding of forgiveness, but rather the event is not perceived as something that needs forgiveness. Nothing "bad" has happened. I may not perceive the event as being very enjoyable, but if I recognize that all things are good – even if I don't see the good or enjoy the event much at the time –I'll be more focused on the good.

I'm not suggesting that you can decide today to see things this way and have it define your life from this day forward. We tend to have habits in our thinking and perception that we've learned over a lifetime. It's difficult to recognize and change habits. But through understanding that our emotions related to an event are based on our perception, and that we can control our perception – we have a choice! We can decide to start living in a different way, and learning new habits and emotional skills.

"No such thing as curses in life"

This is the big lesson that I learned from the challenging experience of the airport community. Several years after we had moved away, I realized that I had grown substantially through the experience. I had developed insights that I might not have developed, had I not had that experience. I noticed, at least in my experience, that the periods when I made quantum jumps in spiritual growth were also periods that were the most painful. Most people have heard the expression "No pain, no gain" so it becomes possible to perceive the pain not as something bad but rather part of the process of growing, which is good.

That's not to say that the pain is a requirement, mind you. I've always railed against that idea – I refuse to believe that the pain is a requirement or even part of the process. Ann had the insight during one of her meditations that the pain is not part of the growing process, but rather the result of resisting change. We all understand, at least intellectually, that change is part of life, but for some reason the tendency is for us to resist the change. I think that must be part of the scarcity mindset – that change is going to bring something Not Good, rather than the Abundance mindset that eagerly anticipates the good that is coming through change. After all, if things are going to get better, they must change from what they are now. Imagine someone who is floating down a river. As they allow the flow to carry them along, they have a comfortable and fun experience, like tubing down the Guadalupe river. If they start trying to hang on to something – to resist the change – they begin to experience the strain of resisting the flow. Their fingers become tired from hanging on, or their arms and legs become tired from swimming upstream. They may get "clobbered" by the logs and other things floating downstream. It becomes a painful experience rather than a pleasant one. It's not the flow that hurts, but the resistance to flow.

It is this realization that led me to create the following saying, and you can quote me on this:

"There's no such thing as curses in life; there's only blessings that we may choose not to enjoy much at the time."

As members of the Unity movement like to say, "It's all good!"

Chapter 10
Spiritual Stages

"Awaiting within us is something beyond our thoughts and beliefs."
— Tyler J. Hebert

Intro to Spiritual Stages

A number of years ago a mentor recommended a book "The Road Less Travelled" by Scott Peck, MD. That book was helpful to me, so as Dr. Peck came out with follow-up books, naturally I bought and read them. One of his later books, "Further Along The Road Less Travelled," contained a paradigm of stages of spiritual growth that I have found to be invaluable. Peck borrowed the concept from the seminal book "Stages of Faith" by James Fowler III, professor of Theology and Human Development at Emory University. I think Dr. Fowler's book was written to torture seminary students – it's a very difficult and dry read. Peck, however, boiled Fowler's seven stages down into four fairly easy to understand stages: Chaotic, Institutional, Questioning, and Mystic/Integrated. I tend to simplify the stages into Stage 1, Stage 2, etc. The concept of the stages is that as people experience life, there are periods where their combined experience leads them to have changing understandings of how the world works and how they should behave. It becomes possible to understand someone's "stage" based on what they believe and how they behave.

An important thing to remember here is that, while there tends to be a progression from one stage to the next as the person grows intellectually and spiritually, one stage is not better than another. They are just different. Let's explore the four stages as Peck describes them.

Chaotic

The first stage, or Stage 1, is Chaotic. Children start out as Stage 1, but most people grow beyond that at some point in their lives. A relatively small percentage of the population remain at Stage 1 into adulthood, say maybe 10 percent. Stage 1 people have not developed a code of ethics for themselves – pretty much anything goes. They can be quite charming, but they can't be trusted, and their life choices often lead to less than desirable results. Stage 1 people can be found in all walks of life and all professions, but they are often identifiable by the trail of disasters they leave in their wake: relationships, living circumstances, scandals and so forth.

At some point the Chaotic lifestyle becomes too painful and the Stage 1 converts to Stage 2 Institutional.

Institutional

The Stage 2 person is quite the opposite of the Stage 1 person. A Stage 2 person tends to be very regimented, with a very rigid code of ethics. Everything is one way or the other for a Stage 2: black or white, right or wrong, us or them. There's no room for discussion, there's no gray area. They accept things on blind faith. People who insist on literal interpretations are pretty solid Stage 2. Keep in mind that for a Stage 2, their "Stage 2-ness" is what is protecting them from the painfulness of the Stage 1 Chaotic lifestyle. The regimentation and rigidity is what keeps them "safe" – anything that threatens the black-and-whiteness is also perceived as a threat to their safety and well-being. Stage 2 people tend to do well in institutional environments where there are clear rules, and there is no question about what is "right" and what is "wrong." By far the majority of the population fall into the Stage 2 category, say somewhere in the 60-80% of the population, and most of those will be Stage 2 all their lives. Stage 2 people tend to be able to tell you the day and time when they had their transitional experience.

Questioning

The challenge is that the world is not black and white. The world is created in glorious technicolor! Many things cannot be interpreted literally. Much of language, literature, and even objects and events in the world contain symbolism; in fact many things contain many levels of symbolism. The Black-and-Whiteness begins to break down.

A good example of this is Biblical interpretation. Even though a Stage 2 will insist on a literal interpretation of the Bible, there are places where the text contradicts itself. So how does one reconcile where this part says one thing, and that part says exactly the opposite? The challenge is that there is much symbolism and metaphor in the Bible. There's only two places where Jesus actually comes out and says something literally, while the rest is couched in parables. On top of that, the Bible as we know it was passed down through rote recitation for centuries, and when it was written down it was often copied by scribes who were illiterate or clergy who at times allowed their own personal agenda to influence their "version" of the copy.

So, at some point a person may begin to see the chinks in the "black and white" armor. The black-and-whiteness just doesn't work for them anymore – they cannot accept things on blind faith. They begin to question anything and everything, testing it to see whether it has the ring of truth or not. Scientists tend to be Stage 3 – they are comfortable with things that they can see, touch, and feel; things they can measure. An important thing to understand here is that Atheists and Agnostics tend to be Stage 3 people. It's not that they aren't spiritual, just that the traditional Stage 2 expression and experience of spirituality doesn't work for them.

Mystic/Integrated

Just as the world is not strictly black-and-white, there is much of the world that cannot be seen, touched, or felt, although to a degree they can be experienced. At some point, a very few people begin to recognize this and be comfortable with the mystery of the world. The questioning becomes less important, the experience of symbolism and metaphor in the world becomes more understandable or at least more acceptable. The urgency of the questioning-ness goes away.

When Ann and I were on our honeymoon on St John USVI, we came across a document called "Rules For Being Human" in one of the shops, pinned to the bulletin board. You can find this document by googling the title. It starts off with "You will receive a body." We liked that document so much that we borrowed it to take across the street to the post office where the only public copy machine on the island could be found, made two copies, and returned the original. That document was helpful – and amusing – to us for some years, but eventually it came to be old hat, and less useful to us. I believe what happened is that the document is very Stage 3, and as we began to grow beyond that, it became less important to us.

My observation is that very few people have moved into Stage 4. I'd guess maybe 1%, or maybe even less of the population has moved into Stage 4.

Rules of the Spirit

Using the Paradigm

An important thing to understand about this paradigm is that the transitions from one stage to the next tend to be painful. It's the painfulness of the not-workingness of the stage that the person is in that drives them to the next stage. People tend to be content where they are, and resist change: they tend to stay in their comfort zone. But at some point the comfort zone no longer exists, and the pain forces them to change. For a Stage 2 person, it's the discomfort of the Chaotic lifestyle that pushes them over the edge. The failed relationships, the jail terms, and so forth just become too painful, and so they embrace the regimented lifestyle that "protects" them from the pain of the chaos. A Stage 3 person transitions when the contradictions and inconsistencies become too much.

A big challenge is that, for a Stage 2 person, a Stage 3 is indistinguishable from a Stage 1. They look the same: they distrust authority, they reject the rules and decisions that are thrust upon them. A Stage 3 person is truly frightening and threatening to a Stage 2. It's not that they intend to be so, it's just that the Stage 2 feels they're being dragged back into the Chaos. It's scary! The other side of the coin is that a Stage 2 person is just as threatening to a Stage 3. The rigidity and inflexibility of the Stage 2 threatens the freedom that the Stage 3 has created for themselves. The Stage 3 feels like they're suffocating in a straitjacket. Stage 2 and Stage 3 people are like oil and water – they don't get along with each other.

I have found the understanding of Peck's Stages paradigm to be very helpful in my daily life, especially with respect to the understanding of the friction between the stages. If I can learn to recognize a person's stage, I can adapt my behavior to avoid their fears and help them be more comfortable with the conversation. If I don't understand this paradigm, I risk driving the person into fear, and the fear shuts down any opportunity to have meaningful conversation or for me to teach the person new concepts and ideas.

4 Stages... and beyond!

The shortcoming of Peck's paradigm as I see it is that it stops at Stage 4. I can understand this: Dr. Peck based his condensation of Dr. Fowler's model on the people that Peck observed in his psychiatric practice and his experience in the world. However, as an engineer I've learned to extrapolate things beyond the limited set, so I believe that the paradigm may – and probably does – extend beyond Stage 4. I mentioned that the percentage of population for Stage 4 was quite small, maybe 1% – one in a hundred – or less of the population. If there is such a thing as a Stage 5, and considering that the population between Stage 2, 3, and 4 has dropped off quite rapidly, what would be the percentage of Stage 5? One in a thousand? One in ten thousand? Would I even recognize someone who is a Stage 5, based on the assumption that I have not yet achieved that level? What would a Stage 5 look like; what would be its characteristics? It's understandable that Peck might not have included a Stage 5 in his model if he never saw one or was not capable of recognizing one when he saw them. If the stages go beyond Stage 4, how far do they go? What would a Stage 6, or 7, or 15 look like? What would their percentage of the population be? What stage was Ghandi, Muhammed, Jesus, or Buddha? I find these questions to be quite intriguing.

Chapter 11
Next Steps

"You will rise, and you will fall, you will get discouraged, you will become encouraged, but always you will be progressing, always, and so you must simply stick to it and the day will come when you will no longer say 'I hope, I desire, I pray,' but you will say 'I know.'"
— Ernest Holmes, Love and Law

Romans 12:2 says "Do not conform to the pattern of this world, but be transformed by the renewing of your mind." This book has provided for you a framework for understanding what is "of the world." I encourage you to begin examining both your own behavior and of those around you in light of this paradigm. Is the behavior spirit-based, or world-based? How would you behave differently if you were to follow the Rules of the Spirit? How might you live according to those rules in the midst of and in spite of those around you who are living by the Rules of the World? Try using the Rules of the Spirit in your daily practice and see how it influences those around you. Don't tell them what you are doing, just do it! Understand that you will be trying to break old habits and form new ones, and it will take some time before you become proficient in the new mindset. If you tell those around you what you are doing, their observation becomes an assessment of whether or not you are consistent between what you are doing and what you are saying, which sabotages the whole effort. I also recommend reading the books mentioned in this book, especially the "Road Less Travelled" series.

Paul McKinley

You might want to sign up for coaching services, or if you have a group that might benefit from this message, I am available as a speaker. Both of these services are available through my website RulesOfTheSpirit.COM. Check back from time to time for new offerings!

About the Author

Spiritual teacher and author Paul McKinley was born in Virginia and educated at the University of Texas, where he earned a Bachelor degree in Mechanical Engineering. Mr. McKinley has had a widely varied career starting as a water-well pipe-stabber, motorcycle mechanic, research assistant, and engineer. As an engineer he worked on projects ranging from designing computer equipment to robotic aircraft part manufacturing to automating bowling ball manufacturing. He moved to providing computer support and eventually worked 15 years as an independent consultant providing expertise on High Availability Clustering.

When he was twenty-two his brother Mike was killed in a helicopter crash, which started him on a lifelong journey of spiritual discovery and enlightenment. For a time he served as a Methodist Layspeaker, before being introduced to the Unity movement at a screening of the movie "The People Vs. The State of Illusion" by Austin Vickers at Unity Church of the Hills in Austin TX. He served as a rotational speaker for Unity of Temple in Temple Texas before moving back to Virginia, where he is a member of Unity of Charlottesville.

Paul currently lives in Virginia, where he teaches about spiritual concepts, especially forgiveness, as well as running a computer business providing computer, network, and internet presence support for local small businesses, and working in real estate restoring distressed properties. He is also an energy healer, practicing Reiki as well as a similar method that he developed prior to his Reiki attunement.

Made in the USA
Middletown, DE
03 September 2017